PETER WRIGHT walked the Watershed of Scotland in 2005. It took him 64 days to cover the whole 1,200km, 745 miles, and he was struck by how much of the route went through wild land. He has long been interested in Scotland's natural environment and history, having volunteered with both the John Muir Trust, and the National Trust for Scotland. He has worked for some 20 years developing the Duke of Edinburgh Award in the Edinburgh area, for which he received the MBE. The National Trust for Scotland presented him with the George Waterston Memorial Award for outstanding voluntary commitment. Peter was instrumental in establishing The Green Team, and is now its honorary Patron.

No other journey through Scotland
can give so sublime a sense of unity – a feeling
of how the Nation's various different landscapes link
together to form a coherent whole.

Ribbon of Wildness

Peter Wright
ISBN 978-1-906817-45-9 PBK £14.99

The next big wild walk…

If you've bagged the Munros, done the Caledonian Challenge and walked the West Highland Way, this is your next conquest.

Ribbon of Wildness provides a vivid introduction to the Watershed of Scotland, which has hitherto been largely unknown. The rock, bog, forest, moor and mountain are all testament o the Watershed's richly varied natural state. The evolving kaleidoscope of changing vistas, wide panoramas, ever-present wildlife, and the vagaries of the weather, are delightfully described on this great journey of discovery.

Peter Wright has done lovers of wild places a great service and providing the first comprehensive description of the Watershed.
THE GREAT OUTDOORS

No other journey can give so sublime a sense of unity – a feeling of how the nation's various different landscapes link together to form a coherent whole.
THE SCOTSMAN

Walking with Wildness

Experiencing the Watershed of Scotland

The Guide to 26 Selected Day or Weekend Walks
Upon Scotland's Watershed

PETER WRIGHT

Luath Press Limited

EDINBURGH

www.luath.co.uk

With fond appreciation of the many influences of KAR,
and in particular:

'...*The hills have, quite simply, given me a lot of good fun.*'

First published 2012

ISBN: 978 1 908373 44 1

The paper used in this book is recyclable. It is made
from low chlorine pulps produced in a low energy,
low emissions manner from renewable forests.

Printed and bound by
Martins the Printers, Berwick upon Tweed

Maps by Jim Lewis

Typeset in 10 point Sabon by
3btype.com

Contents

Preface

'CLEARLY YOU ARE having a love affair', was one of the early comments that I received in relation to *Ribbon of Wildness,* but this was then quickly qualified by adding: 'with the landscapes of Scotland'. I was of course delighted to receive such as observation about the book, or rather, about what the book seemed to represent; about all that had led up to its creation. For it wasn't written on a whim, even after that epic journey from one end of Scotland to the other, but rather it had grown out of a deep and enduring passion for our natural environment, evidence of our interaction with it over the centuries, and our true enjoyment of it now. And as with any love affair, there would be the hope that from that present enjoyment would emerge a deeper affection and care for it in the future.

Walking with Wildness has been written quite simply to provide some of the information necessary, and the further inspiration, to enable more people to get out there and enjoy all that the landscapes of the Watershed of Scotland have to offer, for it is our ever bounteous artery of Nature. There is plenty of space up there, it is unlikely that it will ever get to be crowded, so either solitude, or fellowship within the natural environment, is assured.

But like all good things, it does need to be cared for, so there is a job to be done in calling up the *community of interest* we can all share in the conservation of the Watershed. Whether this is fanciful thinking, or genuinely worth doing, well, there's a choice to be made. But as you read through these pages it is to be hoped that you will then feel motivated to experience some, or all of the walks outlined, do have a great time; do enjoy it, and then perhaps share the pleasure you have obtained with others.

A word or two of thanks are most certainly due here. Firstly to Gary Robbins for his invaluable help in finding a way of producing the 26 route maps. And to my wife Janet for her immense patience.

Introduction

ONE OF THE FINEST and wholly uncompromising delights that the Watershed of Scotland brings is that it is where it is, quite simply because nature alone put it there. Formed out of all the immense forces bound up in geo-glacial time, its place and scale in our landform has been consistent since at least the end of the last ice age. Its identity as a single *geographic feature* may be very recent, and owe just a little to my first book, *Ribbon of Wildness – Discovering the Watershed of Scotland,* but that merely represents a bit of catching up with other islands and continents, and their appreciation of their respective watersheds. Now that ours has been plotted, described and mapped in full, the evidence gathered, and a conclusive argument developed for its key place and continuity, there is much to celebrate about it. Chief amongst this is nature's singular role.

As a route for walking, in whole or in part, the point about the origins of the Watershed, and the lack of human influence in either its making or design, is distinctive, and gives it special appeal. There is something immensely liberating in following a route created entirely by nature; in being guided by the hand of nature, as it were.

That was certainly my own experience when I walked the whole 1,200km of it in 2005, for I had worked out the geographic credentials of the route, and felt that this would stand scrutiny, in every respect. I had looked objectively at the destiny of rainwater falling on Scotland, and then the imperative of its journey by bog, burn and river, to either the

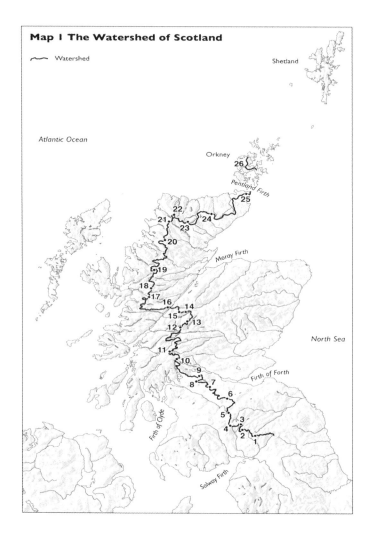

Map 1 The Watershed of Scotland

Watershed

Shetland

Atlantic Ocean

Orkney

26

Pentland Firth

25

22
21
24
23
20

Moray Firth

19

18
17
16
15
14
13
12

North Sea

11
10
9
8
7
6
5
3
4
2
1

Firth of Forth

Firth of Clyde

Solway Firth

Atlantic Ocean or the North Sea. I had considered some key geological factors, and I had taken into account the relatively recent evolution of Scotland's landform, especially as it affected Orkney's transition from peninsula to archipelago. And I was able to say with confidence that although geography may be a discipline created by the human need for order, it helps us in no small measure to make sense of what nature has given us. So the very concept of a Watershed is something that many people have enthusiastically warmed to; it does provide a unique route worth exploring further on foot.

As we explore and experience the Watershed of Scotland, we find that it has a number of particular characteristics that set it apart, in addition to its singular creation, that is. Its average elevation of some 450m above sea level puts it generally on the higher ground throughout, and getting near to the conventional upper limit for commercial tree production; a crude measure, I do acknowledge. That almost 88 per cent of it is Class 6 and 7 in terms of potential land-use, and therefore having very limited, or no use agriculturally, is indeed noteworthy. The proportion of the Watershed that is already protected as Sites of Special Scientific Interest (SSSI) or other designation stands at a remarkable 27 per cent, through almost 90 sites. Every single national environmental agency and organisation has an active presence on it, in one or more locations, or by working in partnership. These factors in particular mark out the Watershed as something special, in more than just quasi-environmental terms. Add to this the very little habitation on and about the route – very few people live thereabouts, with the exception of the one and only settlement, Cumbernauld, and it is evident that it is largely a big long almost uninhabited emptiness. But therein lies so much of its appeal.

Now there arc of course a great many physical and geographic features that bear the hallmark of nature; every hill, river, loch, and bit of coastline show the same stamp. Each and every one in its place or part can be enjoyed for that. Where the Watershed stands out from this though is the scale of it, and its largely wilder character throughout its very long meander through Scotland, end to end. One critic had this to say of it: *'no other journey can give so sublime a sense of unity – a feeling of how the Nation's various different landscapes link together to form a coherent whole.'*

The appeal of the Watershed as a route to be walked builds.

Having extolled its many virtues, it does have to be acknowledged that very little of it is in a truly natural state, but that is of course true of almost the entire Scottish landscape. The human legacy in terms of settlement, farming, felling, hunting, forestry, communication, enclosure, and so much more is widely evident. So the use of the word *wilderness* is most certainly avoided. But it would be true to say that the Watershed does represent a swathe of Scotland's landscape that is in a state that has had relatively less human influence and impact than much that is on either side of it; it is continuously the least affected, the most naturally evolved perhaps.

The author has been busily engaged in an extensive talks and events programme throughout Scotland. These started prior to the publication of the first book in this quartet, and have continued without a break to the present, and indeed well ahead into 2013. Almost 100 very diverse and appreciative organisations have taken up this opportunity, and the feedback is that it has added something of value to their respective programmes. These events have of course contributed to the growing book sales, but they have increased popular awareness and appreciation of the Watershed and of its distinctive character too.

As a route to be walked, this unique geographic feature has immense promise, but it also presents a major challenge or two. For not only are parts of it extremely remote, and call for a fair degree of skill in self-reliant walking and climbing, but its sheer scale would daunt all but the most intrepid. Few could find the time to cover the huge distance involved in doing it end to end, and the logistics involved in walking it in smaller sections may be complex. As a linear route, much of it does not lend itself to day or weekend ventures, for at the end of each outing, the walker will find themselves a long way from their car or transport home, and re-tracing your steps never has much appeal.

With all this, and much more in mind, *Walking with Wildness* has been written to provide a short guide to some 26 day or weekend walks upon the Watershed, which are eminently possible, and are presented in such a way that the transport issues are satisfactorily dealt with. So the reader can now be armed with the information necessary to plan and carry out a significant number of do-able walks, and to get all of the pleasure and fulfilment which this will undoubtedly bring.

Some areas on the Watershed do lend themselves to fairly straightforward days out – where there is a natural loop in the route, as it swings round the headwaters of a single river. There are a number of such features at various locations along the way, so the potential walker will find within in these pages, advice on where to park, and from that, how to get ready access to and from the Watershed – the aim in this being, wherever possible to maximise the *Watershed experience*, and minimise non-Watershed time. But there are not really enough of these 'loops' to provide anything like a comprehensive guide, so a bit of inventiveness has been called for, sometimes presenting a figure-of-eight route. These have been carefully planned to include particular features or points of interest, whilst maximising to the full, the Watershed experience. Some of the chosen routes will either make for a long and quite demanding single day, or could easily be tackled as two slightly shorter consecutive days, with an overnight camp or where possible, a bothy night. At least two of the walks could only be tackled as weekenders, and quite demanding ones at that. There are some in which the use of public transport will be a ready benefit. Finally, some of the walks present an unconventional route round all or part, of otherwise quite familiar mountain features.

The author acknowledges the positive part that a small number of very resourceful people have already played in walking, and indeed running, *their* Watershed, and promoting it in their respective ways. In particular Colin Meek, with his most appealing blog: www.watershedrunning.tumblr.com of 2012, which provides a special insight to the experience and demands of running the whole route in a single four week epic. Dave Hewit's *Walking the Watershed* of 1994, which is now out of print but is available on-line, is a very worthy precursor, and can be seen as sowing the seeds of this walking or environmental genre.

There are others who are now taking up the challenge and experiencing it in their own particular way.

Using this Book and Walking with Safety

The Five 'Marches' of the Watershed

In my earlier publication, I identified five distinct sections for describing the Watershed, and chose to call them 'Marches' – the word march being synonymous with a *boundary*, for that is what much of it is. The Marches are bounded by key geological features, whether fault line, or landscape transition. So the first and most southerly of these is the Reiver March, from the border with England on Peel Fell, to the Southern Uplands Fault just south of Biggar Common. The second is that which crosses the rift-valley of the central belt, the Laich March – laich meaning *low*. This extends to the Highland Boundary Fault near Balfron. The third March takes the Watershed close to the centre of Scotland and is thus the Heartland March, running to the Great Glen Fault. The word moine has two meanings, firstly it refers to a *bog* or *morass*, and it is of course the name of a major geological feature, the Moine Thrust which runs close to the north-west coast. The Moine March is therefore the fourth in this succession. And finally, the Northlands March is self-evident, as it spans the flow country of Sutherland and Caithness, ending at Duncansby Head – the name being inspired by the passion and writings of Neil Gunn. In time a sixth will be added – the Viking March across Orkney and Shetland.

The notes on equipment, personal outdoor skills and

general organisation may offend those who already have the necessary experience, and are equipped in every respect for all that *Walking with Wildness* has to offer. Bear with me please, for I am certain you would think it remiss of me not to remind everyone of what they will need for where they may be going, and just some of the obstacles they may encounter; this all calls for a bit more than just enthusiasm.

Maps and Planning

The maps that I suggest walkers use, and I give the relevant sheet numbers for each walk, are the Ordnance Survey (OS) Landranger 1:50,000 series. These provide the minimum information needed for safely tackling and navigating any of the walks, and putting the route into its wider landscape context. There are a number of other options including digital downloads and printouts, GPS based and mobile phone uploads. And of course the 1:25,000 series has much more useful and interesting detail to be pored over. Conversely however, it must be stressed that the sketch maps in this book are in no way intended as adequate for navigation purposes; they are but a series of useful cartoons. Of necessity, these route maps are not drawn to a consistent scale.

So the point is clearly made that whatever the walkers' preference, with technology or otherwise, there is a minimum standard required for both safety, enjoyment and appreciating the wider surrounding landscapes.

The distances for each walk are given in kilometres, with the approach first, then distance on the Watershed in bold, and exit last, all in brackets, thus: (4 : **14** : 8). The timings are approximate, take some account of varying terrain, and the likely walker's rate of travel. They do not include meal breaks or camping time, but are purely for walking time. Each walker is advised to adjust these prior to departure, by way of intended route plan.

Equipment

When it comes to equipment, there are as many possibilities and personal preferences as there are puddocks in a pond; every walker will have their own favourites, theories, and prejudices. No harm in that of course, but it has to be stressed nonetheless that Scottish hill and mountain conditions can be both demanding and unpredictable, and walkers, whether solo or in a group, must be fully equipped for all eventualities. To be otherwise is simply irresponsible, and may well endanger others. There are plenty of good sources of information and advice; the outdoors shops, websites and magazines are all avidly competing for everyone's attention – and money. It is down to each walker or group to formulate their own kit-list, and be aware of why they have selected each item, or rejected others. It is also down to each walker to know how to make safe and best use of every item of equipment.

So that is by way of a necessary word of caution, but from personal experience, it is one of the enduring truths of the hill and mountain experience that having the right gear will contribute much to the enjoyment of the outing. There is something very re-assuring about knowing that you are as well-equipped as you need to be, and can then get on with the business of enjoying the venture, appreciating the surrounding landscapes, and interacting with nature. Every walker will have a tale or two to tell about great days out, and more.

Skills and Competence

Now it wouldn't do for this author to preach about the nec-essary levels of competence in outdoor skills for anyone who is intending to tackle any of these day and weekend walks. Suffice it to say however, that the walks vary in length, ter-rain and potential exposure. None should be underestimated, but each and every one can give a truly fulfilling experience. All of the couth sayings about 'proper planning' hold true, and will favour a successful and safe outcome. Do be aware of your physical fitness, and from that, your likely rate of travel. From experience, there is nothing dignified in having to be Mountain Rescued, no matter how uncritical your rescuers may appear to be! Assuming that you are fully pre-pared and well equipped, I would say that the two key skills that you *must* have are good navigation in all conditions, and a fair competence in route finding; in short, sound mountain-craft.

Obstacles

Much of the route of the Watershed of Scotland is off-track – it is most definitely not a recognised Long Distance Route (LDR) – yet, so be prepared to reconcile the map and the terrain effectively in order to be sure of the correct route. Fencelines may help in this, but they must not be depended upon – they are there to keep animals in or out, not mark a walking route. The same can be said of such tracks as there are, in that they will have been created or evolved solely to suit those who work in the hills and countryside.

Fences will almost certainly prove to be an obstacle on

most, though not all, of the walks. I give good sound practical advice in my earlier book, on how to safely traverse every kind of fence without damage to yourself, your expensive clothing, or the fence (it is there for an economic purpose), and without loss of dignity. For some obscure reason, fences seem to become more severe the further north that you travel; those in Caithness and Orkney may prove to be quite challenging! Wherever possible do look for a gate to use or climb over (at the hinges end). I list the likely number of fence crossings for each walk. Fences are not however, permanent features, so walkers will need to be prepared for either additional fences which have been erected more recently, or find that some have been removed. The number of fences listed is therefore not definitive.

‘Beasts’ is the vernacular word for cattle, in the farming community, at least. There are a few places where these may be encountered. They will in all probability be of beef cattle breeds, and therefore not normally aggressive (their curiosity is another matter) – though cows with small calves would be the exception.

Bog will at times frustrate, and slow you down; many’s a wide sweep will be necessary in order to get round the stuff. My advice: no heroics – stay dry shod if at all possible.

If you come across a flock of sheep with young lambs, you would be advised to give them a wide berth; I would sympathise with a shepherd, if she/he shouted at you for blundering through the middle of it. Sheep are not the brightest, but they will be part of somebody’s livelihood, so that merits respect.

Similarly, deer and the stalking season should be taken into account. The hill phones network will give access to information about intended stalking on specific estates and dates. It is strongly recommended that this service is utilised.

Terrain

Although the walks have been selected wherever practical to avoid steep ground and craig, this has not always been possible, so be prepared where necessary. The direction in which the walk is being advised has not been a random one. It is much easier and safer to go up a steep area than it is to descend.

Crossing rivers and burns on either the access or exit to the walk may be necessary, and wherever possible the routes are set out in such a way as to make use of bridges where they are believed to exist. The author has gone to some length to research this, but acknowledges that the information may be out of date to the walkers' advantage, or disadvantage. Where water crossings are necessary, care is needed, and it may be prudent to make a small detour in order to find the safest and most practical crossing point.

Mobile Phones

Most of the routes set out in *Walking with Wildness* are predominantly on the higher ground, and so mobile reception will generally be good on the more popular networks. But this cannot be taken for granted, so self-reliance will be wise at all times.

And finally: a brief quote from the Outdoor Access Code

- Take responsibility for your own actions.
- Respect the interests of other people.
- Care for the environment.

These three principles have been agreed upon following much discussion and debate involving all relevant interests, and thus provide a sound basis for responsibly enjoying the countryside.

In the Spirit of it All

WERE YOU TO ASK many walkers and climbers what they get out of their chosen activity, most would talk readily and even passionately about the experience with nature which it brings; that it's not just about getting the top of the hill, but very much about the journey too. As we pick a route round, over or through any feature that nature has provided, so we begin to interact with that landscape. As we observe all of the colour, texture and movement, the sounds and smells, the warmth or cold, and as we react to that which a journey inevitably brings, so we are affected by it. If our pace is unhurried, we will surely tune-in to what is around us – not just what is ahead. It is often deeply personal, but each in our own special way is enriched. Whether it is simply the contrast with the everyday experiences, or something more profound, we are uplifted by it; our spirits are raised, or even soar.

A walk on the Watershed surely offers an almost limitless supply of this eco-spiritual bounty; the largely continuous wildness, the more naturally evolved landscapes, the promise of solitude with nature – that very force that created it, and just the simple knowledge that once you are on the ribbon of wildness, you are plugged-in to an immense artery of nature running the length of the land. No other geographic feature on this scale has such promise.

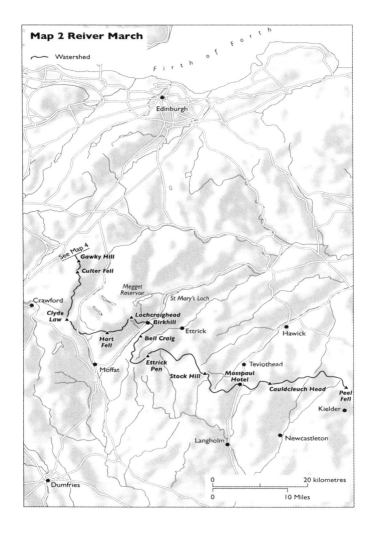

Map 2 Reiver March

Watershed

Firth of Forth

Edinburgh

See Map 4

Gawky Hill

Culter Fell

Megget Reservoir

St Mary's Loch

Crawford

Clyde Law

Lochcraighead

Birkhill

Ettrick

Hawick

Hart Fell

Bell Craig

Ettrick Pen

Moffat

Stock Hill

Teviothead

Mosspaul Hotel

Cauldcleuch Head

Peel Fell

Kielder

Langholm

Newcastleton

Dumfries

0			20 kilometres
0		10 Miles	

The Reiver March (5)

THIS IS A LANDSCAPE which resonates with historical interest, where the marks of earlier deeds and events are never far below the surface; their echo is heard within contemporary popular local celebration. Roman, pilgrim reiver and drover all found their way through these glens, stagecoach and railway ran their respective courses, and both sheep and plantation in their turn have displaced indigenous peoples. It is a place of evolution and change, but the hills stand proud.

Here in these rolling Border and Moffat Hills, as the Reiver March of the Watershed meanders from Peel Fell to the Southern Uplands Fault, it marks a route that survives the encroachment of Wauchope, Craik and Eskdalemuir Forests. It rides majestically round the headwater hills above upper Ettrick, Moffat, Annan and Tweed waters, and ends with a fine overview of the lowlands' central belt.

Over 130km in length, and at an average elevation of some 550m, the Reiver March includes three designated areas – two of which are Special Areas of Conservation, and all are SSSI. With only two houses on it, there is an uninhabited feel to it, and the five roads that cross by, have little impact.

Although these hills and the five walks which are offered here are little more than an hour from the big centres of population, they are all too often overlooked in favour of more dramatic terrain further north. This is regrettable, because here is truly fine hillwalking country, and the Watershed encompasses some of the best of it. Generally firm underfoot, the going is fair, the views are fine, and there is an appealing sense of place. In clear conditions, The Cheviot, the familiar profile of the Lakeland Fells, and the widening expanse of the Solway Firth, are amongst the rewards to be had. And time can be enjoyably spent picking out landmarks across the Tweed Valley, with the Lammermuirs as backdrop. Access to these hills and the outings proposed is easy.

Walk I   In the Rolling Border Hills
Sheet 79
Distance 26km (4 : **14** : 8) – 10 hours
Access by car or bus

'These Rolling Hills' is the description often applied to so much of the uplands south of the Southern Uplands Fault, and it is most apt. The Watershed is central to this; it is on the higher ground throughout and forms the horizon in many places. Its character and profile is of generally rounded hill forms, rarely is it craggy, but rather, it seems to just roll gently from one hill to the next. There is probably a direct link between this lack of drama, and its' general emptiness. Although within easy reach of a number of the main centres of population on both sides of the Border, a walker could easily venture out for several days and see few if any fellow travellers.

The A7 is one of the main north-south routes through these hills, and the Mosspaul Inn sits a mere half kilometre off the highest point on this road. The hills around it are certainly rounded, and largely free of commercial forest; they have great appeal, and much to commend them. This walk will include Tudhope Hill (599m) to the east of the A7, with Comb Hill (513m) and Ewenshope Fell (493m) to the west.

Obstacles   4 fences, sheep, and the possibility of beasts.

The Approach

Travel on the A7 to Mosspaul Inn and park. Cross the road, go through the gate facing you, and turn left alongside the fence until you pick up the old track leading past Braehead

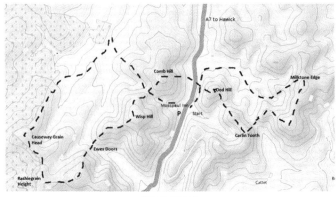

Route Map 1

cottage. Skirt the woodland just beyond the cottage and turn right to pick up the track leading past Elygrain. Bear left onto the track leading towards Millstone Edge (567m), where you join the Watershed.

The Walk

The Watershed has reached this point by way of Cauldcleuch Head and Greatmoor Hill, on a route with open moor and hill to the right, and commercial forestry to the left. Further back, it has followed the remains of a fence line through the forests, as a narrow survival of more natural and unplanted terrain.

Turning right along the fenceline to Tudhope Hill (599m), the ascent is not arduous. The Descent to spot 483 and the crossing between Linhope Burn and Carewoodrighope Burn is somewhat steeper, but it is on firm grassy terrain, and in season, the wild flowers are a joy to see. These crossings on the Watershed, normally marked with a gate, were in earlier times, of some importance, as they often represent the shortest route between settlements on either side of the high ground. More recently, they have provided a means whereby stray sheep can be returned to their home farm and hirsel.

Carlin Tooth (511m) beckons; a prominent, if otherwise unremarkable hill. The word Carlin refers to a *witch* or *old hag*, so the name is evocative and most certainly descriptive. It is worth noting that further north, in the more ragged Highlands, a hill like this would not stand out in any way. But here in these uplands, it has a distinctive character. A right turn on to Bye Hill leads towards Dod Hill; dod or dodd, being a *bare* or *rounded hill*. The next target, clearly visible across the other side of the crossing that carries the A7, is equally descriptive – Comb Hill (513m), the *'bosom among the hills'*. Its appeal has however been somewhat compromised by the 100m high steel mast sticking out of the top of it. In summer there is bracken on the slopes on both sides of the A7, so at the end of the day's walk, a tick-check will be advisable. These tiny black parasites can be the bearer of Lymes Disease, so their speedy and effective removal from (the crevices of) the human body is a must. The upper reaches of the steel marred 'comb' is over heather, and briefly, slightly rougher terrain.

Even if thirst is needing quenched and a rest would seem appealing, it is worth waiting the extra time to get to Pikethaw Hill (564m) by way of Wisp Hill (595m), Ewenshope Fell (493m) and Ewes Doors. This latter is a reference to the start of the Eweslees Burn, which becomes the Ewes Water. Meanwhile, on the other side, the strangely named Wrangway

Burn poses more questions than it provides answers. And the ascent from this ancient place is rather more demanding than we are used to as yet. So rest atop Pikethaw Hill, brew-stop calling, and take in the views; Teviot and Tweed one way, with Eskdale and Solway the other. The Eildon Hills will stand out amid the gentle Tweed Valley, The Cheviot may be discernible on a clear day, Peel Fell, and where the route of the Watershed of Scotland started can be identified by the clutter of masts atop Deadwater Fell to its right. There is a hint of the outline of Lakeland Fells, and Criffel just to the south of Dumfries is a faint marker for the Solway beyond. Westwards from here, a wide expanse of Craik and Eskdalemuir forests is only relieved by the patchwork which the areas of felling or re-planting have created.

But it is time to move on, with Rashiegrain Height (507m), Corbie Shank, and Causeway Grain Head in sight. The upper reaches of both the Wrangway Burn and the Giddens Cleuch, come almost to within touching distance of the Watershed, and are part of the river Tweed SSSI. Round to the left above the forest edge is Whitehope Edge (477m), and the end of this section of the Watershed is almost in sight at the very head of the Teviot, marked by the Teviot Stane. The vegetation on this final stretch is ungrazed, in places it has grown rank and represents quite tough going, but it contains a rich mix of plantlife and wild flowers. And for sheer enchantment, the sound of the skylark will fill the air with its rich melodies.

The Exit

There are two choices for the return to Mosspaul Inn. Either pick-up the forest track close to the Teviot; go to Gideonscleuch, cross the moor to the track that leads to Langhope Height and Comb Hill. Contour to the right before the summit to the coll between it and Wisp Hill, and follow the burn down to the Inn. Alternatively, retrace to Corbie Shank, and turn left to Haggis Side and Merrypath Rigg, to pick up the Langhope Height track.

Walk 2   The Ettrick Horseshoe
Sheet 79
Distance 26km (3.5 : 18 : 4.5) – 11 hours
Access by car.

Often referred to as 'The Ettrick Horseshoe', this route is a classic amongst the well-recognised walks in this area; that it is on the Watershed provides much added interest, and gives it a distinctive place in the wider landscape. As a loop in the Watershed, that runs for almost 20km on the hills round the headwaters of the upper Ettrick Water, access is relatively straightforward, and it provides an opportunity to experience something of the continuous wildness that so characterises the Watershed. The walk offers two choices: to tackle it as a quite demanding single day venture, or to split it over two consecutive and shorter days, with an overnight in either in Over Phawhope bothy, or wild camping. But in spite of it's ready access and appeal, it is rarely busy – walkers will enjoy a fine sense of solitude throughout much of their outing. Whilst navigation is fairly easy and the terrain is generally firm underfoot, it nonetheless requires good clothing and equipment, and competence in their use. The route is not without hazards in places.

The prominent hills of Ettrick Pen (692m), Bodesbeck Law (665m) and Herman Law (614m) all form part of this fine uplands outing.

Obstacles   3 fences, sheep, and no beasts.

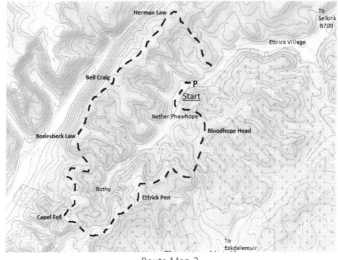

Route Map 2

The Approach

Travel from Selkirk on B7009 and then B709 to Ettrick Village, bear right onto the unclassified (U) road and continue 5km to Crook Cottage, which is on the right. Park your car on the hard-standing at grid reference point 219125 on the left just before the cottage. Walk 1km along the road, to cross the Moffat Water on the bridge to Nether Phawhope, continue east, ascending by the rough track to Black Knowe, and then south to join the Watershed on Bloodhope Head (535m). Note that Over Phawhope farm is due to be ploughed and planted with trees in 2012–2013, and the terrain may change as a result of this. The Watershed has come up to this point from the south east from Eskdalemuir Forest by Pentland Hill and Cross Hill.

The Walk

So you are now on the Watershed of Scotland; ahead lies a fine walk, and much more besides. Some of it will be obvious, and some require a bit of interpretation, but in any event it promises much. Do take your time and experience it to the full.

There are three distinct sections to this loop: From Bloodhope Head to Hopetoun Craig, to Bodesbeck Law, and finally from there to Herman Law. Whilst the one factor which all share, is the valley of the Ettrick Water and all of its tributary burns to the right, the landscapes and wider vistas to the left of each are very different.

The first section, which I will call the Eskdaleside, gives wide easterly views over the vast commercial forests of Eskdalemuir, Craik and Wauchope, with the distant skyline taking in Peel Fell and Hartshorn Pike. The northern skirts of this immense green cloak slope gently into the middle reaches of the Tweed Valley, whilst the southern orientation is Solway bound. In places, the sitka and larch plantations lap close to the Watershed, indeed, at the boundary stone in the col between Bloodhope Head and Mitchell Hill, it is confined to a narrow ride between two blocks of planting. A little further on, the areas around the Muckle Cauldron Burn are more open. Although some of the detail has been obscured by forest, a look at the 1:25,000 Explorer map shows a plethora of intriguing names – Swang Bog, a Coomb or two, a Kip and Buzzard Linn, Blaeberry this and Rowantree that, and somewhere in amongst it all, a Gutter and a Syke.

These and so many other very descriptive words provide some insight to how our ancestors viewed or experienced *their* landscapes. We can find our own delight in it too – look out for the micro habitats that have formed on some of the rotting fence posts, with lichen, mosses, blaeberry and heather all finding it amenable. With the unplanted land left ungrazed by sheep for several decades, the vegetation has in places grown rank and tussock strewn. Some varieties of wild flower can't compete in this environment, and have been crowded out. But on the more open slopes, they are in abundance.

Atop Ettrick Pen, which was formerly known as The Pen of Eskdalemuir, are the remains of an ancient cairn which gives a tantalising hint at the significance of this place long ago. It is ours to enjoy now though, for the wide views, the sense of place, and at 692m a real feeling of elevation over all that is around.

Navigation on this route is not especially difficult, but proper equipment and the ability to use it is essential. Although much of it follows a fence line, there are a number of 'fence meetings' that might just confuse.

Ettrick Head would seem to be the most fitting name to give the second section, from Hopetoun Craig round to Bodesbeck Law. The valley to the right has closed in, whilst to the left, the burns and ridges radiate outwards from our Wind Fell, Capel Fell and White Shank. The vistas from here are southerly and softer; the few hills in the foreground soon give way fields and the Solway beyond. Looking across to the great chasm that is Black Hope, there is both a sense of contrast, and of what is yet to come.

The Southern Upland Way passes at the col, where a

sign advises that to cross, would be to enter Dumfries and Galloway – follow this LDR far enough in that direction, and you'll reach Portpatrick, or turn the other way, and it is Cockburnspath that awaits. This place gives a particularly clear image of the Watershed and it's Atlantic : North Sea divide. Just 2km down the track to the right, Over Phawhope bothy will be found – a fine establishment of its kind. It lies in an amphitheatre of hills, where no man-made light can be seen at night. On a moon or starlit night it has a magical atmosphere. On the left, just before the summit of Capel Fell, a 300m gash in the hillside has been washed-out by heavy rainfall; it is big enough to be named on the map as Rae Grain.

Well before White Shank is reached, the Watershed is marked by a very fine drystane dyke – the Great Wall of Ettrick, perhaps? After the Bodesbeck crossing, a steady ascent of 180m brings the journey to the summit of Bodesbeck Law (665m). The scene changes dramatically at this point.

The valley of the Moffat Water differs greatly from the upper Ettrick. The latter is typified by the rolling hills which surround it, and the gentle ridges which spread out from them. The Ettrick Water sweeps in a number of wide meanders as it progresses from its source towards the influx of the Tima Water at the village. The valley of the Moffat Water on the other hand has been carved long and straight by immense glacial action; a powerful and dramatic formation. It would be tempting to call this section of the route Mirk Side, for that is indeed what the steep slope to the left is called – a place where the sun doesn't reach it at all in winter. Instead, I will choose a name with an element of mystery to it – Andrewhinney. Who was he, and why a hill named after him?

This final 7km on the Watershed here, is formed of a

succession of ten identified tops, all in excess of 600m, and rolling easily from one to the next. The going is good, and offers ample opportunity to compare the different terrain to left or right, and perchance to seek out the occasional moss pool with its dancing light and reflections. Time to see the bog cotton dance too in the passing breeze and in season to appreciate the rich moor grasses varied hues. The eye is quickly drawn to the succession of deep glacially sculpted land forms on the other side of the Moffat Water, with Saddle Yoke, Carrifran Gans and White Coomb standing bold like a majestic guard of honour. But the full enjoyment and experience of that is for another occasion (see walk 30). Today, Andrewhinney and his neighbours provide a ridge walk that is almost without equal in the Southern Uplands.

The Exit

Herman Law is the finale to this particular outing on the Watershed, and of the three fences that meet here, one has been our guide, the one at right-angles to the left of it would take the route down steeply to Birkhill and the A708 crossing. If visibility permits, take a bearing instead for Peel Fell, for that direction will lead down onto Standtrae Knowe and Cossars Hill to the south east, and Brockhoperigg cottage. Just over 1km on the road will then take you back to your car before Crook Cottage.

Tall White grassed hilltops crawling with voles, with sleekit sneaky creatures down big shingly holes.

Sights down lochs, commanding views far and wide,

unpredictable weather that makes the hardy hill sheep hide.

Steep challenging slopes accomplished with pride in bonnie Ettrick hills your memory will abide.

Calum Flemming
The (contemporary) Ettrick Shepherd, on Over Kirkhope.

Walk 3   Round the Upper Moffat Water
Sheets 79 and 78
Distance 27km (4 : 19 : 4) – 12 hours
Access by car

This walk is filled with interest and includes both terrain and features that have considerable popular appeal. Three major environmental organisations play an active part over two sites, and with much of a 2,2850ha SSSI within the bounds of the route, it is rich in montane and sub-montane species, and designated as being of National importance. There has been major geological and archaeological discovery on and about the Watershed hereabouts. And today's para gliders enjoy the challenges and rewards to be had in jumping off its tops.

This will be a demanding one day walk, both in terms of overall ascent and distance. It could be tackled as a lighter two day venture with an overnight wild camp at Loch Skeen, or in the fairly basic Gameshope bothy. A further alternative would be to split the walk over two separate days, with Birkhill as the start or finish of each day; this would require two cars (see below). The terrain, though steep in places, is generally good underfoot. Much of it is grazed by sheep, some feral goats, and there are rough paths in some parts. The need to climb over fences is limited to perhaps two locations, where there are no alternatives. Good clothing, footwear, equipment and the ability to use it are essential. The general advice is, do not underestimate this walk.

The Watershed forms a loop round the head of the Moffat Water, making access to it short, but relatively steep on both the original ascent, and the final descent.

This walk takes in a number of delightful hills, including

Firthope Rigg (800m), Lochcraig Head (801m), Andrewhinney Hill (677m) facing the Grey Mare's Tail, and Bodesbeck Law (665m).

Obstacles   4 fences, sheep, and no beasts.

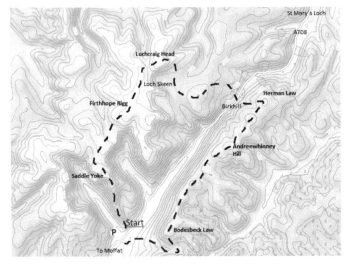

Route Map 3

The Approach

Travel on the A708 from either Selkirk or Moffat and park your car at the small layby for the Shepherd's Memorial beside the Spoon Burn bridge at 154105. There is another tarmac layby on the river side of the road about 200m downstream. And in summer weather there may be grass verge parking close to Blackshope cottage.

Using the stile in the fence on the up-side of the Spoon

Burn, cross into the Borders Forest Trust's Carrifran Wildwood property. Follow the rough path that zigzags up the hill onto Saddle Yoke – this is a 565m ascent. Follow the inside of the boundary fence onto the top of Raven Craig, where you will join the Watershed of Scotland. At this point it has come east from the Devil's Beef Tub by way of Hart Fell and Hartfell Rigg.

The Walk

The terrain splits into three distinct sections – the higher ground from Raven Craig (and indeed the earlier Saddle Yoke) to Lochcraig Head, from there to Herman Law, and the final 7km to Bodesbeck Law. In marked contrast to the Upper Ettrick Water walk, this one is deeply and steeply glaciated on the inside of the loop, but characterised by rolling hills around the outside.

Rotten Bottom is, in one sense at least, a paradox, because it is not at the bottom, but near the top. That said, crossing it is not without challenge – teetering along the top of the sheer craigs, leaping from one area of seemingly firm grass to another, or the inexorable deep hag-scarred peat: take your choice. But it is the Watershed, and it was here that the Rotten Bottom Bow was discovered. The Carrifran Wildwood is a visionary project to re-create an entire valley forest as it would have been 6,000 years ago. The Borders Forest Trust, with the support of the John Muir Trust and others had the vision, and the fruits of the first half million trees to be planted, are beginning to re-establish the cycle of regeneration. So, the landscape is changing, the biodiversity is rapidly increasing, and a rich environmental legacy for future generations is being formed. The Watershed's eye view of this is inspirational. As you emerge from the fenced area, it is well worth seeking out one of the stiles or gates in order to exit – that fence has an important and expensive function.

To the left, two reservoirs which supply some of Edinburgh's need for drinking water catch the light and a plethora of mysterious hill names give but a glimpse into the life and work of our forebears. Whilst on the Watershed itself, the going has improved, as from Firthhope Rigg and onwards to Lochcraig Head, there is almost a path to be followed. Overgrazing by sheep here is however, damaging the vegetation and general ground cover. It is indeed a great pity that the ambitious bid for Talla and Gameshope Estate which the Borders Forest Trust and the John Muir Trust had pulled together was beaten by someone or some company with deeper pockets. Here the route now bounds the National Trust for Scotland property which is popularly known as the Grey Mare's Tail. Take time to pause then, on Lochcraig Head to appreciate the vistas of hill, valley, and moor that seem to roll on inexorably round three points of the compass, to far horizons. Loch Skeen fills the craig-ringed hollow some 280m below: it is amongst the highest hill-lochs in Scotland.

From Lochcraig Head to Herman Law is a mere 5.5km, but there is both variety and interest to be enjoyed along the way. The descent towards Loch Skeen hints at the need to visit its shore, for the contrast between water and enfolding craig is beguiling; the detour is well worth it. If this is to be the spot for an overnight wild camp, then there are practical matters to be attended to. There is a good likelihood of spotting some of the small flock of feral goats that live in the vicinity.

The covenanting period in our history is marked by Watch Knowe, for it is believed that the name relates to its use as a lookout point. Set back from the pass, and with the rough uneven moorland round it, it would have given good cover for watchers, and the field of vision included all of the upper reaches of the pass – both Moffat and Yarrow bound. At Dob's Linn, one Charles Lapworth made his graptolite discovery, which provided one of the turning points in our understanding of the Earth's crust and geological evolution. Whilst making these discoveries, he stayed at Birkhill, which was at that time, a small Inn. The Birkie Cleuch which ascends steep and deep to Herman Law beyond gets the birk part of its name from the traditional name for a birch tree. It was one of the very few locations in the wide area where they flourished, out of reach of the voracious sheep. Herman Law is a turning point, but before you turn, saviour the views northwards to Loch of the Lowes and St Mary's Loch, with Tibbie Shiels Inn as a white dot amongst the trees betwixt the two. Look east and you can pick out Peel Fell on the distant horizon – just to the left of the hill with a clutter of masts on its summit.

The final section of this Watershed walk is along a fine ridge with ten named tops on it, all around or just over the 600m mark, and providing a magnificent walk south west to Bodesbeck Law. Contrasting the gentle rolling hill and valley scene on the left with the dramatic hillscape on the right is breath-taking. One main glacier carved and ground its way down towards Moffat Dale in a clear straight line which left the flanks of this ridge steep and rock-bound, and with no sun to warm it in winter. Three side glaciers gouged the hollows of Skeen, Carrifran and Blackhope, and left a guard of honour in the form of White Coomb (the highest hill in this area), Carrifran Gans and Saddle Yoke. It is an impressive scene, by any standards.

The walking on this ridge is generally firm underfoot, navigation is straightforward, and the succession of cairns, like markers on a high-way. The descent from Bodesbeck Law to the crossing track at the forest edge is not difficult, and it is here that you leave the Watershed. Were you to continue on it, it would take you to White Shank, Capel Fell, and the full round of the Ettrick Horseshoe.

The Exit

The path down to Bodesbeck Farm is clear, and easy to follow. Cross the ford just before the steading, go through the gate ahead of you, and with the steading and older house on your right, walk to a junction in the tracks. Turn right, cross the Moffat Water by the farm bridge, exit onto the A708 close to Capplegill, turn right and walk back to your car.

Plan B

This requires two cars. Leave one at either Birkhill (beside the mast or old forestry gate), or at the Spoon Burn layby, and take the other to the start of your walk. There are a further two choices, both of which will make for a good day out on the Watershed; either Birkhill and Herman Law to Bodesbeck Law, or Birkhill and Lochcraig Head to Raven Craig.

Walk 4 The Devil's Beef Tub

Sheet 78
Distance 16km (4.5 : 8.5 : 3) – 7 hours
Access by car

The Devil's Beef Tub conjures grim and fearful images – of Satan himself perhaps, or of dreadful deeds by some malevolent character in the murky past. For most people, the DBT is seen from the A701 and the safety of car or coach. Even from this vantage of passive appreciation it looks awesome enough though. The Watershed runs right along the very lip of the chasm which Sir Walter Scott described as 'A d—d deep, black-guard looking abyss of a hole.' Where better then, than to experience the place, than from around and upon the Watershed?

The highest of the hills on this walk is Hart Fell at 808m, and then includes Whitehope Knowe (613m), and the more modest but still dramatic Great Hill (466m).

Obstacles   2 fences, no sheep, and no beasts.

The Approach

Drive north out of the centre of Moffat to the roundabout at the former Moffat Academy building, go straight on along Beechgrove, and travel about 5km to a public car park on the right just before Newton. Locate a sign for Hartfell Spa, and follow the footpath close to the Auchencat Burn, ascend Arthur's Seat, followed by Hart Fell where you join the Watershed. It has come to this point from the east and north from Lochcraig Head by way of Raven Craig (see walk 3).

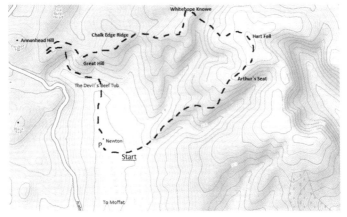

Route Map 4

The Walk

At 808m Hart Fell is not quite the highest hill hereabouts – White Coomb beats it by less than 20m. But Hart Fell is impressive in its own right. The views to the south are far reaching and draw the eye over a very wide area of Annandale, and towards the Solway Firth. The Border with England lies somewhere over to the south-east, and Galloway may be seen beyond the forests to the west. A number of landmarks stand out and beg to be identified. Moffat lies in the cusp of the hills to the south of this great vantage point. Another chasm can be seen disappearing over the Craigs (all of them have names to ponder) into Black Hope to the south east. Just to the north lies Ask Law, but this may have less to do with a question, and more to do with a newt, for the traditional name for newt, was an ask.

46

The only things to mar this landscape are the intrusive meeting of the fences, and the recently constructed wind farm beyond Clyde Law to the west. But the rim of the Devil's Beef Tub, and its place on the Watershed awaits.

Being sure to pick the right fence line for the descent, the first goal is Whitehope Knowe. It quickly becomes evident that there is a marked difference between what is happening on the two sides of the Watershed here; a difference that will become yet more dramatic. The old footpath from Fruid crosses at Spout Craig – we may experience more spouts on at least one walk further to the north. There is as always, so much in the names of surrounding features, and Crown of Scotland is surely intriguing. It was here that in 1306 Robert the Bruce forged an alliance with James Douglas, which resulted in Bruce becoming king; an unassuming place for a very significant event in our history. At the point where the path crosses, a well-built drystane cairn points the way downwards for the Annandale Way. But we continue to Chalk Rig Edge.

The landscape to the left of here is slowly changing, with the recent genesis of another Borders Forest Trust initiative. Corehead Farm, which extends from the valley floor to the Watershed and the route of today's walk, is being planted with native trees, and already the evidence of a richer bio-diversity is showing positive results. Although there are similarities with Carrifran, here there will be more of a patchwork of planting, and it is being used more extensively for training purposes. Corehead will not reach its potential in my lifetime, but in that of my grandchildren, it will become something to really enjoy; the trees will have a huge impact.

Ironically Great Hill is over 40m lower than Chalk Rig

Edge, but it stands out much more boldly, louring even, over the deep hollow that is the Devil's Beef Tub. A further path crosses just beyond, leading from Earlshaugh. Recent proposals for a wind farm there are being strongly opposed by a range of environmental, tourist, and landscape organisation. They are right to oppose such a plan, for it is nonsense in such an iconic location. I gladly add my own words of condemnation, and very much hope that as people read this in the future, they will find that the idea has been abandoned forever. The ground to the north slopes gently towards the hills above Fruid Reservoir; moorland that changes so subtly from season to season, but is perhaps best in the autumn with the deep reds of the moor grasses.

Annanhead Hill may seem to be a good turning point, but it is well worth continuing round the forest to the north to Flecket Hill. The mast is a distraction, but at this point you are just above the source of the River Tweed. Down there in the mosses the Tweed's Well starts what will become further downstream, a truly majestic river; and every metre of it, starting here at your feet is one very long SSSI.

Go back towards the corner of the forest, and down the track to your right. This will take you through the forest to a point just short of the A701, turn left, back onto Annanhead Hill, and down to the Earlshaugh path. At this point turn right, and leave the Watershed – at the source of the River Annan, so close to the start of that other great river.

The Exit

Follow the path round the flank of Great Hill, to Corehead Farm and thence back to your car just beyond Newton.

Walk 5   Coulter Fell and Gawky Hill.
Sheet 72
Distance 21km (7 : 11.5 : 2.5) – 9 hours
Access by car

A walk that has two of Scotland's major river systems close-by on either side of it is unusual. The two rivers, each iconic, though in very differing ways, are the Tweed and the Clyde, and this particular Watershed walk looks down from its heights on both. Indeed, this is the only location on the entire Watershed where this phenomenon occurs. Whilst there are places where river sources are close together, like those of the Spey and the Roy further north, here, the rivers are well formed, and their respective valleys give wide vistas to hill and moor furth of their margins.

This walk is designed to maximise the use of the Watershed's meanderings to give a really fine day out on the hill, whilst having good access at both ends. The astute will note that there are two spellings of the same name marked on the map; the Fell, Farm and Kirk are all Culter, but the village is Coulter; a pleasing conundrum to muse over.

With Culter Fell (748m) as the high point on this walk, it also includes Gathersnow Hill (688m), and Scawdmans Hill (573m), with some surprisingly deep cols between.

Obstacles   1 fence, sheep, and the possibility of beasts on the lower ground.

The Approach

Drive along the A702, and turn onto the U road on the north side of the bridge in the middle of Coulter village. Continue

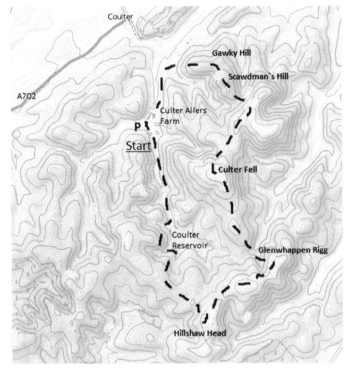

Route Map 5

for 3km to Culter Allers Farm, and park on the roadside just beyond. Walk south to the track that turns off to the right just before the Reservoir, which will take you onto a shoulder leading up to spot 534. Turn south east, and climb to join the Watershed on Hillshaw Head (652m).

The Walk

To get to this point, the Watershed has followed all of the tops along the west side of the upper Tweed Valley; from Clyde Law, Powskein Dod, Wills Cleuch Head, and by Coomb Dod – a fine walk in itself, if two cars are available. The fence line is a good guide, and generally follows the Watershed. Whilst the going is good, there are areas of bog, where a wide deviation of up to 50m may be either prudent or necessary. Gathersnow Hill gives easy walking on short vegetation, and at Glenwhappen Rigg, where there is a sharp left turn, take time to absorb the views to the west over rolling hills punctuated by reflected light from a few lochs and reservoirs. To the north east, the valley of the Holms Water draws the eye towards Broughton, which is variously famed for the John Buchan connection, a delightful cottage garden, and for the popular output of its brewery.

The steady descent to Holm Nick needs a degree of concentration, but the terrain, though steep is not rough. A 260m ascent by Moss Law takes the Watershed up a long shoulder onto Culter Fell. Time and place for a brew-stop, for the views are spectacular here too. To the North West, another spur of the Fell is aptly called Fell Shin, and the next outpost is Tippet Knowe – a reference to a witch, or perhaps even a coven of them! Some obscure royal connection is alluded to here, with steep sided Kings Beck to the left, and the next top, which is King Bank Head.

Turning left before Cardon Hill, the descent is yet again steep and steady, and thankfully on grass and close cropped heather. No sooner down, than back up again onto Scawdmans Hill, before curving round on a track, to the hill with two names; Gawky Hill, or Black Hill. To gawk, means to stare, so do take the hint, for this is a place of marked transition. Although the Southern Uplands Fault lies a little beyond, its edge eroded and thus obscured by many years of activity, this is the point on the Watershed where its existence is most evident. South and east of here, the way we have come, and the hills are in general a good 300m higher than the floor of the rift valley which lies to the north and west. This fault line, which runs in one clean sweep from Ballantrae to Dunbar, represents a sharp divide between upland and lowland. Whilst the Watershed beyond here somehow swings from one rocky outcrop to the next, takes in moor and such higher ground as there is, it almost survives proud of the cultivated areas, and retains its relative wildness throughout what I have called The Laich (low) March.

The Exit

Continue westwards to spot 499 and to the ancient fort beyond the Nisbet Burn. Turn left and onto the track through woodland that leads through Culter Allers Farm and the U road. A further left turn will bring you back to your car.

The Laich March (4)

THE WATERSHED HAS a much more troubled journey to make across the rift valley of the low or laich, central belt. Here, is seemingly so much more to confuse and obstruct its wildness. But wildness there is, and in surprisingly good measure.

The average elevation of the Laich March is 280m over its 175km meander from the Southern Uplands Fault just south of Biggar Common to Gualann on the Highland Boundary Fault, close to the south east corner of Loch Lomond. The character of this March is immensely varied, but the notion of relative wildness holds. Moor and rough grazing predominates, with two key areas of hill in the South Pentlands, and Campsie/Gargunnock Fells. The few scraps of arable land are generally punctuated by hedgerow and blocks of woodland.

The route through Cumbernauld, the one and only settlement on the entire Watershed, is marked by areas of woodland, ancient hedgerow, and more recent planting – never more than a hundred paces from greenery. The Watershed here provides a very redeeming image for this often (unjustly) maligned New Town, and will hopefully generate an asset worth nurturing and even celebrating in the future. In addition to this one settlement, there are only a further 15 or so houses on and about the Laich March.

The Laich March can boast 14 designated and protected areas, including SSSI, Special Area of Conservation, Ramsar, and Special Protection Area. It includes the only Countryside Park on the Watershed, and the valuable work carried out by the Central Scotland Forest Trust has contributed much

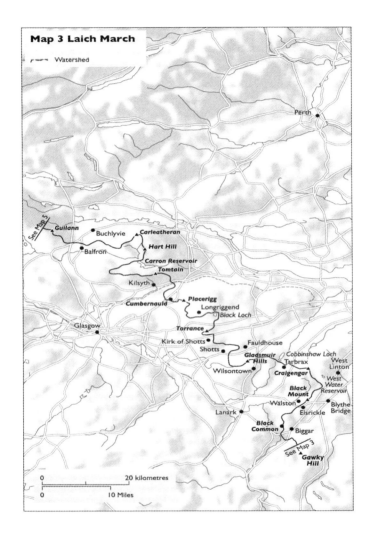

Map 3 Laich March

- - - Watershed

Perth

See Map 5
Guilann
Buchlyvie
Carleatheran
Balfron
Hart Hill
Carron Reservoir
Tomtain
Kilsyth
Placerigg
Cumbernauld
Longriggend
Black Loch
Glasgow
Torrance
Kirk of Shotts
Fauldhouse
Shotts
Gladsmuir
Hills
Cobbinshaw Loch
West
Linton
Tarbrax
Wilsontown
Craigengar
West
Water
Reservoir
Black
Mount
Walston
Blythe
Bridge
Elsrickle
Lanark
Black
Common
Biggar
See Map 3
Gawky
Hill

0   20 kilometres
0   10 Miles

to the greening of the area – not least upon the Watershed. Areas of former industrial blight are slowly being reclaimed for nature by nature, through a potent if gradual combination of neglect and with an occasional helping hand from conservationists.

Whilst the four walks that are proposed in the Laich March do exploit some of her finer opportunities, the perspectives which they give on the wider landscapes are positive too. Reading about them may just prompt some of the people living in the central belt, and the thousands who cross the Watershed daily, to ponder, and then to 'don their boots. For as this geographic feature crosses the rift valley it is the giver of much, and most surely merits both appreciation and protection.

Walk 6 Across the South Pentlands
Sheet 72
Distance 20km (7.5 : 12 : 0.5) – 7 hours
Access by car or by bus, and on foot

Anything that the south Pentlands may lack in terms of grandeur is compensated for in many other ways: the beauty is often in the detail. As a walk on the Watershed, it encompasses some key locations in the wider scheme of things. This walk involves crossing the Pentlands directly from Garvald to Bawdy Moss on the old Covenanter's Grave path, and returning along the Watershed.

Access from Edinburgh in particular is straightforward, and the other major centres of population are within easy reach. If there is one thing to be on the alert for, here, it is deception! A number of features could all too easily confuse, or even lead you astray. In any event, it is a good Watershed day out.

The trio of Craigengar (519m), Fadden (466m) and Catstone (448m) form the core of this more gentle hill day.

Obstacles   3 fences, sheep, and some beasts.

The Approach

From the A702 at the north end of Dolphinton, drive about 1km up the U road signposted to Garvald and Dunsyre. Park at the road-end to Garvald, opposite the former sand quarry. Walk up the Garvald road and join the Watershed at about 487101. You will return to this location at the end of the Walk. To reach this point the Watershed has crossed the low ground, and come from Black Mount by way of White Hill.

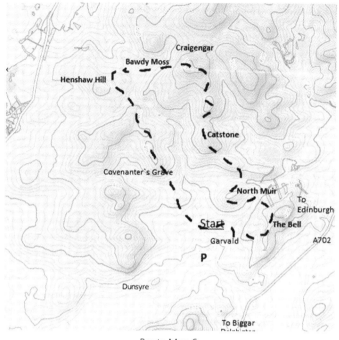

Route Map 6

Follow the road into and part way through the Garvald settlement, and in the farmyard look out for a right of way sign for Crosswood. On the far side of the field in front of you, a footbridge, constructed by Friends of the Pentlands, will take you over the Medwin Water, and further signage will direct you up the east bank of the West Water. The right of way path takes a pretty straight route by Black Law, the Covenanter's Grave, and skirting White Craig on the right and Henshaw Hill on the left. You will reach the Watershed at grid reference 065547 almost in the middle of Bawdy Moss. You will be turning right towards Craigengar, but it is worth noting that the Watershed heads west and north from here by Maiden Hill, Crosswoodhill and the south end of Cobbinshaw Reservoir.

The Walk

You start on a SSSI which includes 320ha. of Bawdy Moss and Craigengar. The former is noted as being upland raised bog, and the slopes of Craigengar are dry heather moorland. There are no landmarks or features to identify the Watershed between the two, so it is necessary to read and interpret the landscape, and to reconcile what is on the map, with the terrain. The longer your legs, the better you will be able to deal with the tussock and bog; the word Moss is deceptive – it may be 'soft', but it can be hard going. If you are lucky, you'll find a trail of flattened vegetation where an All-terrain Vehicle (ATV) has been. There is no dubiety about the wildness here! The word 'bawdy' traditionally refers to a *hare*.

The slopes of Craigengar are firm and the going is good. Near the top a fence line from the right is met, and leads decisively to the summit. This is a place to appreciate at a number of very different levels. Firstly, the views along the flanks of the Pentlands towards Edinburgh are fine indeed, West Lothian opens up to the north, and Lanarkshire fills the vista to the west. Black Mount stands out clearly to the south, and the hills including Culter Fell, on and beyond the Southern Uplands Fault make for a horizon that demonstrates by comparison the lower elevations of the Laich March across the central belt. Not only is Craigengar a SSSI, but it is also designated as a Special Area of Conservation (SAC) for its dry heaths, marsh saxifrage, and species rich grassland. Geographically, it is the point where the Watershed bids farewell to the River Tweed catchment which started, in terms of the Watershed at least, away back on Hartshorn Pike, close to Peel Fell. And finally, it is the point at which the vast area of operation for the Central Scotland Forest Trust starts. Craigengar is no ordinary hilltop.

The descent is from the second of the two cairns, to Fadden and Catstone, with a sweep to the west between the two. Bulldozed tracks are never things of beauty, and they may or may not have their uses on this walk; they will tend to draw you away from the Watershed in places, so reading the landscape is the guiding principle. West Water Reservoir just to the east has triple designation as SSSI, Ramsar and Special Protection Area (SPA) citations. Before the ascent to North Muir, another of those leg-sapping mosses has to be negotiated. From North Muir, the Watershed then swings well to the left, then right to The Bell, and left again towards Mendick Hill – the north side of which is another of those SSSI's. The route then turns towards Garvald by moor and fields that are used primarily for grazing. Fences, gates, and sheep with young lambs do need to be given some care here, before the point on the Garvald road is reached once more.

This walk is not in any way dramatic, and parts of the terrain are frankly abused – for the purposes of grouse shooting. But it is special in a number of ways that have been identified. On a recent outing on it in the middle of winter, I found that some of the rich green mosses were active, a small light grey-green lichen that has the seeming delicacy of coral was a delight to see, and another mid-grey lichen had tiny bright red buds less than half the size of a match head, to marvel at. Such heather as does survive is in season, vivid.

The Exit

Return to your car by the U road.

Walk 7   The Watershed View of Cumbernauld
Sheets 65 and 64
Distance 14km (1.5 : 12 : 0.5) – 6 hours
Access 2 cars or 1 car and bicycle

One of the outstanding qualities of the Watershed is it's emptiness; it's generally uninhabited nature makes it almost unique. There is however one settlement that does straddle it, and which calls for a closer look, if for no other reason than that it is the only major habitation. For other than the New Town of Cumbernauld there are fewer than 25 houses on and about the entire 1,200km of the Watershed of Scotland. Cumbernauld has been maligned, not so much for the rest of it, but on account of one collection, or sprawl of buildings, clustered around the so called 'Civic Centre'. No comment on that is needed here, but it is necessary to say that much of the rest of the Town is well designed and has some environmental qualities that would be the envy of many more established urban areas. Trees and woodland are at the heart of this good planning.

As the Watershed of Scotland meanders its way through the Town, it seems to link up a number of areas of old or established woodland, new planting and suitably neglected old hedgerow. So the walk will hopefully be a revelation, and show one important facet of Cumbernauld in a new and appealing light.

This New Town has been built on what can only be regarded as gently undulating country, and this is reflected in the walk, which has no steep ascents. The elevation varies between less than 100m and 170m.

This is a two car venture.

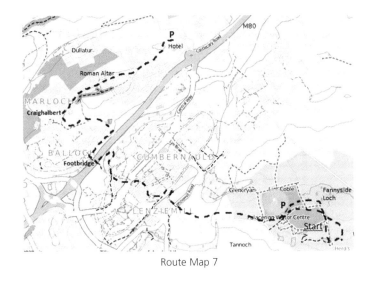

Route Map 7

The Approach

Take one car to the Westerwood Hotel on the north side of the M80 close to the Old Inns Services. Drive in the other car to Palacerigg Country Park on the south side of the Town. Walk south and east from the Park Centre along the track that passes the golf Club House, and on to Fannyside Loch. It is then necessary to climb over one fence to get to Herds Hill, the highest point of Fannyside Moss, where you meet up with the Watershed.

Obstacles   1 fence, no sheep or beasts, some fairly dense mixed woodland.

The Walk

Fannyside Moss is part of a triple designation – the Slamannan Plateau Special Protection Area (SPA), the West Fannyside Moss Special Area of Conservation and the West Fannyside Moss SSSI. Surrounding areas of poor quality landscape belie the importance of Fannyside. The Watershed has reached this point from the moorland surrounding Longriggend and Greengairs.

Return to Fannyside Loch (this is where the easier fence crossing can be found), cross the track, and walk in the rough and woodland alongside the golf course, and heading back towards the Club House. The core of the woodland is sitka spruce with some larch, but it is clear that time is enabling some diversification, with a variety of deciduous trees now taking their place. In spring the bird cherry is an eruption of white blossom against the dark green backdrop. Both the Club House and the Park Centre are almost exactly on the Watershed, both are surrounded by woodland of various types; provide a rich habitat for birdlife, and all that it takes to support such diversity. The journey then heads west through woodland and scrub, and across rough grazing lands of Greenside. This area is scheduled for development at some time in the future, so it is to be hoped that the opportunity will be taken to incorporate something in the plan to respect and even celebrate the Watershed.

Crossing the B8054 the Watershed then passes through a row of small industrial units before dipping once again into rough woodland south of the station. A footpath gives ready access through this, and an old bridge, a safe crossing of the railway. The railway embankments are a fine jumble of greenery, whilst we cross the road, go round a block of flats, and pick up more (rather denuded) woodland running up the hill to pass neatly between two churches. A pedestrian underpass then leads to some planted areas surrounding sheltered housing, before a pedestrian bridge crosses the dual carriageway, and takes the path into yet more mature woodland. Descending past rows of terraced housing, there are odd mature trees and evidence of hedgerow remnants that run down past Seafar School, through another underpass and onto grassland that leads into the woodland that is part of the extensive North Side Wood Nature Reserve run by Scottish Wildlife Trust. A long term objective is to introduce greater species diversity.

Crossing the Motorway calls for a minor diversion by the footbridge, whilst the actual location of the Motorway's crossing of the Watershed is some 300m north east at 751750. Although there is a strip of woodland running up the hill amongst the houses of the Balloch area, there are two equally good alternatives, as the objective here is the old quarry and church at Craighalbert at the top of the hill. Either, follow the woodland alongside the Motorway to the right, and head towards the Cemetery which is surrounded by the visionary Cumbernauld Community Park – an environmental gem fostered by determined local community effort. Alternatively, bear left after crossing the footbridge, follow the path up across an area of grassland, and enter an open block of mature (though dense in places) woodland, which will lead to the old quarry, crossing only a couple of roads on the way. The former of these options is nearer to the actual Watershed. The Church at Craighalbert is on the Watershed.

After a right turn past the slowly emerging Mosque, pick up the line of an old Roman road running along the crest of the hill. Much of the hedgerow on both sides has survived almost as far as the Roman Altar Stone, giving hawthorn blossom, dog rose, and brambles in season. Crossing the roundabout just beyond the water tower, the Watershed then enters a long strip of dense mature woodland to the south of private housing. This area is passable, but requires a modicum of both determination and care, with the clear objective of reaching the Westerwood Hotel. A final hurdle in this adventure is airborne golf balls. But the hotel serves food and refreshments at all times of the day and evening, so a brief interlude before reclaiming the other car, will have been well earned.

Although the Westerwood Hotel may be a welcome diversion, the Watershed has in fact veered north from the Drumcap Plantation to the rough scrub at the near end of the Airport enclosure, and crossed the tree-girt Antonine Wall, the railway, and the Forth and Clyde Canal.

The Exit

Return to Palacerigg Country Park and collect the other car.

Walk 8 Round Carron in the Campsies

Sheets 64 and 57
Distance 21km (5.5 : 15 : 0.5) – 7.5 hours
Access by car

The central belt is of course the most heavily populated part of Scotland, with greater Glasgow in the west, and Edinburgh in the east of the country. In his book *Clone City*, Miles Glendinning predicts that without careful planning, this will all with time become one vast conurbation, engulfing every settlement along the way. Such a depressing scenario might be some way off yet, but thankfully there are a number of locations within this rift valley which would obstruct the advance of such urban sprawl: the Laich March of Watershed. Although it has not quite avoided encroachment, as the last walk illustrates, the succession of hills, rocky outcrops, woodland, bog and designated areas, will with their increasingly precious environmental status, stand apart.

Often rather loosely referred to as the Campsie Fells, there is a tight collection of hills which includes in turn, the Fintry, Kilsyth and Gargunnock Hills, with the Carron Valley and its Reservoir in the midst, all sitting just north of centre-stage. Though perhaps lacking the drama of other locations on the Watershed, three rivers here seem to do battle, to determine the furthest reaches of their respective headwaters. The rivers Kelvin, Carron, Endrick and Forth push the Watershed this way and that, and provide an impressive hilly meander.

A walk round the head of the Carron catchment gives two very contrasting vistas. In a wide sweep to the south, the panorama is generally urban in character, with both cities, and much that lies between them. Turn the corner as it were, on Holehead, and the view is of the upper Forth, with the Highland Boundary Fault line, and the promise of all that lies beyond.

These hills may not be high, in comparison to much that lies further north, but the views that they offer, more than compensate – Garrel Hill (459), Lecket Hill (547m) and Holehead (551m) mark out the route.

Obstacles   7 fences or dykes, sheep, and no beasts.

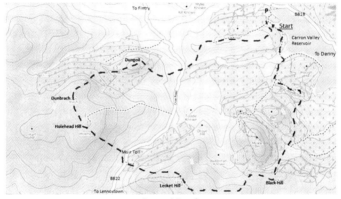

Route Map 8

The Approach

Drive along the B818 to the western end of the Carron Valley Reservoir and park in the car park which is signposted there. Walk south on forest tracks to Black Hill, either by way of Meikle Bin, or the track to the east of it. Join the Watershed at Black Hill.

The Walk

The Watershed here has come from the east by Garrel Hill and Tomtain following a crossing of the Forth and Clyde Canal at Netherwood, but more prudently and dryshod at Wyndford Lock.

Head west over rough moorland, to Lecket Hill where the path which marked on the map both before and after this top is, not quite on the Watershed, but the terrain is fair. It is from this point that the views of the urban aspects of the central belt are most striking, in a wide arc which takes in Falkirk with Edinburgh beyond, Cumbernauld, the major Lanarkshire towns, and of course Glasgow. If conditions are right, the light will catch the modestly tidal reaches of the Clyde near the City centre, whilst to the east the panoramas include the salt mingled waters of the lower Forth. This is but a first and rare glimpse of salt water on both sides from the Watershed. Were you walking the whole route, it is something which would not recur for a very long time, so savour it here.

Having either passed or climbed Meikle Bin en-route to this point, you would perhaps have been fascinated by the Bin family of Meikle, Little and Bairn – a nice touch of humour in the landscape. The wind farm on the other side of the Reservoir is for discussion on the next walk, but it will most assuredly provoke.

The descent over more open hillside to the B822 and a point close to the 'Source of the River Carron', necessitates a route that carries the risk of pine needles down the back of your neck – this wedge of the forest straddles the Watershed. The ascent to Holehead is much less hazardous, and a dyke-line acts as a good guide. An ugly mast detracts from the scene, so do take shelter in the lee of the dyke, look the other way, and have a brew-stop. Farewell to urban vistas, and time to ponder the delights that the next top will bring.

Dropping down to the col between Dunbrach and Dungoil is obstructed by crag and forest, which requires a bit of careful route-finding. The trees were planted in rows, whilst this may be poor visually, it does help with finding a passable route through to Dungoil; time for another brew-stop perhaps.

Although the top of Dungoil has been marooned by the surrounding forest, it provides very fine views to the left along the hills and craigs above Fintry and Ballikinrain. Moving round, the upper reaches of the Forth valley spread out in a patchwork of field, woodland and moss, with a superb mountain backdrop of Ben Venue and The Trossachs beyond the Lake of Menteith. The Highland Boundary Fault, though difficult to locate precisely from this angle, represents a major transition in the landscape none the less. Across the valley of the Endrick Water, Stronend stands out assertively like the bow of a great ship – the name is the giveaway, as it simply means 'the end of the nose'. The blades of the wind farm on Hart Hill to the north east turn easily in the afternoon sun, and the forest fringed Carron Valley Reservoir stretches off to the right. Fine views indeed, punctuated by the light catching the surface of the waters.

Spot 321 is the next goal, beyond the B822, and so, down into a short stretch of forest once again, remembering an earlier comment on the manner in which the trees were planted. In the open, the terrain is reasonable, with a slight swing to the right and the corner of the forest on the opposite side of the road. Some bog ensues, but soon enough the well grazed grass is a delight to walk on, for it is liberally peppered with wild flowers of many kinds and colours. On reaching the top of this hill, which would aptly be described as a 'knowe', in good scots vernacular, the next object is another spot height. Barely rising above the surrounding green forest cloak, spot 307 should somehow be reached, for it is that, and not the forest tracks which mark the Watershed. The dyke, or the fence, which bound the forest is a prior challenge. The end of the nearer track is on a good bearing, but thereafter, the forest rides offer the best hope of reaching 307. On reaching it, the terrain gets a little easier as there is the remnant of some less dense and more mature pine. The views of the Reservoir and of Cairnoch Hill are here framed well between the trunks of these trees, and invite a photo or two. The final steep drop to the forest track and the loch shore brings this walk on the Watershed to an end, formally at least.

Before the Reservoir was created the Watershed would have crossed an area of bog to Sir John de Graham's Castle or *Motte*, as it is marked. But unless you have come armed with a wetsuit, it would seem that to go round by the dam would be the wiser course.

The Exit

Return to your car in the car park at the western end of the dam.

Walk 9   The Gargunnock and Fintry Hills
Sheet 57
Distance 21.5km (1 : 13.5 : 7) – 6.5 hours
Access by car

This walk promises a real sense of isolation from the more urban world beyond, with for part of it at least, a feeling of being in an amphitheatre surrounded by hills. The wide watery expanse of the Reservoir is the centre of attraction, whether it is for calm reflections, or dancing light on a breezy day, its level surface somehow accentuates the rolling line of the hills beyond. This walk also promises fine views across a wide arc from two significant vantage points. And the experience of walking right through a small wind farm will surely provoke contrasting reactions to the need for renewables, the siting of wind farms, and the current economics of wind-borne energy.

Two hills stand out on this walk – Carleatheran (485m) and Stronend (511m).

Obstacles   4 fences or dykes, sheep, and no beasts.

The Approach

Drive along the B818, and park your car in the sign-posted car park at the western end of the dam, at the west end of Carron Valley Reservoir. Walk across the dam, and follow the road east as far as access to the remains of Sir John's de Graham's Castle. Join the Watershed at this point. Strictly speaking it has come to this point beneath the sheet of water, for if we could wind the clock back to the days prior to the Reservoir; it would have crossed a bog from the hill

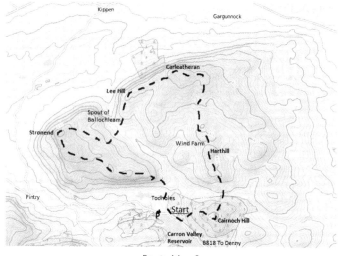

Route Map 9

spot 307, with its clump of mature pines. But we would surely wish to start this walk dry-shod.

The Walk

Access to the castle, which is now just some rough grassy humps, hollows and a few stones, is straightforward, and the curious traveller can find out more about it by reference to the information boards. Then the fun begins! The first summit to be reached on this walk is Cairnoch Hill, and when the forest which surrounds it on all sides was planted, it was clear that access on foot was not a consideration. Recent felling on some parts of the hill has further confused the situation, and makes it easier and more difficult, in equal measure, to get to the top of the hill. This is one of the very few places on the entire Watershed where the route is truly frustrated, by trees, or the remains of them. Action is needed hereabouts to liberate our route.

That said, the traveller will have to make the best of the situation as it prevails at the time, and partial use of forest tracks may be forgiven. The remains of a dyke running across the hill from south to north heralds the start of the clearing on the summit, with its trig point, fine spread of wild flowers and various embankments, which suggest some earlier use or human activity. The views are a delight. But that interlude is soon over, with the need to do battle with the forest yet again. That old dyke line might prove to be a bit of a blessing.

The route is northwards from here to Carleatheran by Hart Hill. Once clear of the forest, a rough tussocky, and in places boggy, patch precedes the U road crossing. By contrast, the hill on the other side is well grazed and easy going and it is well worth aiming for the gate in the dyke which is in the lee of the first wind turbine.

The substantial track that has been imposed upon the moor may seem handy, but it follows an engineered route which deviates in places from the natural route of the Watershed. Whichever way you go though, questions will most surely arise in your mind or amongst your party, as to the rights and wrongs of wind farms. In the first printing of my earlier publication, I was somewhat ambivalent on this issue, though generally siding with the need for, and the broader environmental value of wind power as a key source of renewable energy. Things move on though, the construction of more wind farms on and about the Watershed, and the threat of more to come in what would now be regarded as either environmentally or visually sensitive locations, has shifted the argument the other way I believe. Readers can judge for themselves the position I now take in the Preface for the second and subsequent print runs. Those who follow the issue will have been informed by the role of the John Muir Trust, amongst others in giving a more critical and well-argued approach.

One thing is certain, and that is that this wind farm is here, and will be around for at least the next 30 years. It is most certainly intrusive here, as you wend your way between these arguably graceful white structures. It is worth taking the time however to stand directly beneath the powerfully rotating blades, and get a sense of the energy that is bound up in their seemingly inexorable movement. Look up, and experience the blade as it appears to drop out of the sky towards you, but with a mild passing 'whoosh', it continues its circuit upwards, only to be followed by another and another. All those who argue either for or against this form of technology should at the very least obtain this experience; there is certainly nothing abstract about it.

If plans for this particular wind farm, and indeed any other one on the Watershed were being pursued now, I would undoubtedly argue against the proposal. As the technologies advance on offshore capability, for wave and tidal sources of power, and for many other forms of renewable, it seems that the imperative for land-based wind farms is diminished. I suspect that within a decade we will seriously question the wisdom, the economics, and the visual impact that our current rash of wind farms has had on our landscapes; we will be found wanting by future generations, I fear.

One final factor which I have no doubt whatsoever will in the future have a major bearing on this, is simply, the Watershed and its newly discovered, unique qualities as both a geographic and landscape feature. The case for safeguarding the Watershed and enhancing its wildness is compelling. Wind farms have no place in this.

Once clear of the turbines and clutter, the moorland becomes rougher, and the prospect of reaching Carleatheran is the focus of attention. As you catch site of the ancient cairn, the last hundred metres or so, gradually reveal a widening and deepening panorama. The ground falls away steeply to the north by Black Craig, and then presents in one vast gesture, the entire spread of the upper Forth Valley. To the right, the southern escarpments of the Ochill Hills watch boldly over the tidal meanderings of the final stretches of the River, and as it transforms into the Firth. Familiar features predominate, with Stirling and its Castle, the Wallace Monument, and Dumyat beyond. Draw a veil, if you can, over the Braes of Doune wind farm. All the rest though, is a rich patchwork of woodland, field, moss, loch, and the gentle weave of the River within this fine swathe of countryside. Carleatheran is as rewarding a vantage point as you could wish for to survey all that lies below and beyond. And clearly the ancients found this to be a significant place too, for the cairn that you are sitting on, is a substantial construction that had meaning.

Turning left, or south west, the descent in the direction of the Spout of Ballochleam, is over varied terrain of heather and grasses. The craigs to the right continue the steep drop to the valley below, with a number of big ledges holding small lochans that defy normal drainage conventions. To the left, a huge amphitheatre has opened out with the Backside

Burn and then the Endrick Water draining to the south, almost to the Reservoir, but then taking a very sharp right turn towards Fintry and to empty into Loch Lomond. Ahead, lie the Fintry Hills, dominated by Stronend. The ascent takes a course between the Boquhan Burn (which empties over the spout of Ballochleam), and the Shelloch Burn. The going gets quite rough on this gradual climb, but the pay-back is the summit of Stronend, from where the views are every bit as fine as the earlier Carleatheran.

The north side of the Campsie Fells on the left are steeply sculpted by corrie and craig, whilst due west, the first hill on or just beyond the Highland Boundary Fault can be picked out; Gualann would point the Watershed on its route along the eastern side of Loch Lomond. But to get there, a steep climb down the craigs on the north side of Stronend would be necessary, followed by Kippen and Balgair Muirs, with Balfron Station and the mast at Bat a Charchel along the way. Stronend invites a long last look, before leaving the Watershed and returning to your car.

The Exit

Follow the spot heights on the Fintry Hills and head for Todholes farm. You will pick up the track to the wind farm about 1km before the farm, and this gives an easy stroll back to your car beside the Reservoir dam.

The Heartland March (6)

NO OTHER PART of the Watershed can be seen as offering such widespread popular enjoyment. It includes areas that are the most visited; some readily accessible and others remote. For generations of walkers and climbers, these tops provided their first tantalising introduction to the many and rich rewards of simply being in the hills.

The Heartland March of the Watershed of Scotland starts on Gualann on the Highland Boundary Fault and extends to Laggan on the Great Glen Fault. The journey from one to the other links the two National Parks, circumnavigates much of Rannoch Moor, embraces 16 Munros and nine Corbetts, and spans eighteen designated areas. Four major environmental organisations and partnerships play a part, and one significant estate has signed up for biodiversity. Its 240km at an average elevation of over 600m takes in some immensely rugged terrain, and provides rich evidence of wildness in many different ways.

Many who never even climb a hill will feel a sense of familiarity with much of Heartland, as it is crossed by the West Highland Way at four locations, the West Highland railway line crosses five times, and even the A82 on three occasions. Thousands of people admire and feel affection for these hills and landscapes from car, coach and train, or on foot and by bicycle. With only two houses on the route, the largely uninhabited character is manifest. And as the name of this March implies, it strays close to the very heart or centre of Scotland.

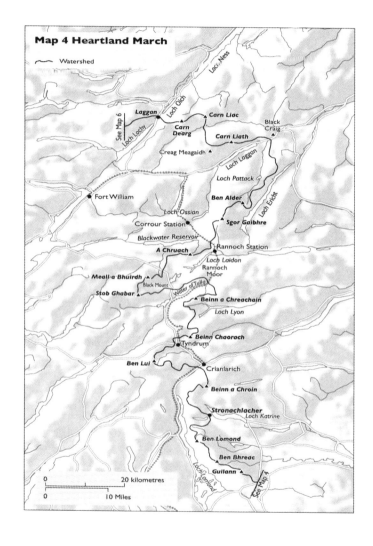

Map 4 Heartland March

⌒ Watershed

Loch Ness

Laggan
Loch Oich
Carn Liac
Black Craig

Carn Dearg
Carn Liath

See Map 6
Loch Lochy

Creag Meagaidh ▲

Loch Laggan

Loch Pattack

Fort William ●

Ben Alder ▲

Loch Ericht

Loch Ossian
Corrour Station ●

Sgor Gaibhre ▲

Blackwater Reservoir

A Chruach ▲

Rannoch Station ●

Loch Laidon
Rannoch Moor

Meall a Bhuirdh ▲
Black Mount

Beinn a Chreachain ▲

Stob Ghabar ▲

Water of Tulla

Loch Lyon

Beinn Chaorach ▲
Tyndrum ●

Ben Lui ▲

Crianlarich ●

Beinn a Chroin ▲

Stronachlacher
Loch Katrine

Ben Lomond ▲

Ben Bhreac ▲

Guilann ▲

See Map 5

Loch Lomond

0 _____ 20 kilometres
0 _____ 10 Miles

The six walks which are here offered, promise a variety of challenge and potential solitude, and the views from many of the heights will both impress and inspire.

Walk 10   The Hills Above Glen Arklet
Sheet 56
Distance 22km (2 : 16 : 4)   9 hours
Access by car

Loch Arklet is somewhat in the shadow of its much larger and more romantically associated neighbour, Loch Katrine. Although many people drive past it, en-route to Stronachlachar, or if they are feeling adventurous, to the road-end at Inversnaid on Loch Lomond side, few will dally for long, to admire Loch Arklet. The Watershed passes very close to its eastern end, across the narrow strip of rough ground that separates it from Loch Katrine. As a feature that is very much within the Watershed's immediate drainage pattern, it has a thoroughly confused purpose though. Originally, as a much smaller Loch, it drained directly into Loch Lomond, and is therefore on the Atlantic side of the picture. For the past 150 years though its waters have been dammed and commandeered, along with the much enlarged Katrine, for Glasgow's water supply. Katrine traditionally drained into the Forth and is therefore eastward draining, to the North Sea. So the waters of Arklet went west and Katrine went east, but together, as water supply, they both cross the Watershed at Bog of Ballat near Balfron, and are consumed in Glasgow, only to end up (having been purified) in the Clyde and heading west. Hence poor Arklet's confusion.

Confusion or no, there are some fine rugged hills around the shores of the Loch, which carry the Watershed on its elevated journey, and which form part of this unique east:west divide. This walk, which many will find to be quite demanding, exploits the opportunity which this partial loop provides, and gives us the first venture into a rocky landscape; in a glimpse perhaps, of much that is to come.

Beinn Uamha (596m) is the higher top on the south side of Loch Arklet, and the ragged northern side is marked by Maol Mor (684m)and Beinn a Choin (770m).

Obstacles   4 fences, few sheep, and no beasts.

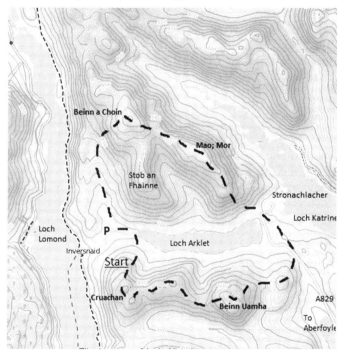

Route Map 10

The Approach

Travel on the B829 north west from Aberfoyle to the view-point and car park just before Inversnaid. Climb Cruachan (536m) immediately to the south-east of this, and continue to join the Watershed at 354074 just beyond Lochan Cruachan.

The Walk

The Watershed has reached this point along all the hills on the east side of Loch Lomond, and in particular from Ben Lomond and Cruinn a'Bheinn. Loch Arklet below now provides a fine foreground, for the ragged array of hills on the north side which will form the more demanding part of this walk. Their summits are all crag-rimmed (with what I earlier referred to as 'rocky doodles'), and they are separated in dramatic fashion by the steep sided valley that holds the Corriearklet Burn. The contrast between this rocky prospect, and the three major lochs to left right and centre is striking, impressive even. But we have some 5km of business on this side of the valley to experience first, traveling east to Maol a'Chapuill (515m) and Beinn Uamha (596m), with Gleann Gaoithe *valley of the wind*, below to the right. Descend to spot 392 by skirting the north end of Lochan Mhaim nan Carn, and follow the forest edge to get as near as possible to spot 184 on the road.

Cross the road and onto the rough ground which sepa-rates the two lochs – the surface of Loch Arklet is some 33m higher than that of Loch Katrine, so the water flows unaided from one to the other. Garradh (559m) *the dyke*, is the next target, and will present a hard pull up the 400m of ascent, calling for a fair degree of skill in route finding in order to avoid the craigs and scrub woodland. Continue north-west to Maol Mor (684) *big bald head*, and take a breather for the views are magnificent. Loch Katrine with its heavily wooded shores swings away boldly to the south east, and points the eye to the Trossachs and its Queen Elizabeth Forest Park. This is clad in a dark green cloak of pine, which is enlivened with a number of lochs – Chon, Achray and Vennacher to name but three. Ben Lomond triumphs over the view to the south. Much of the area around is protected or designated in some way, a number of key agencies are working together on ambitious woodland regeneration, and the Watershed sits astride the Loch Lomond and Trossachs National Park. It is an exceptional area, beyond the Highland Boundary Fault.

Few walk these particular hills, for there are bigger and more challenging peaks to the north and west, so solitude hereabouts is almost guaranteed. A solo walker will surely feel one-ness with nature – that great enhancement of the human spirit which wildness so richly shares.

The route to Beinn a'Choin (770m) is amongst and over a wild jumble of craigs and slabs which might conspire to draw you off course and into difficulty, so close navigation is essential. In between these outcrops, the vegetation is rough, and makes for slow progress. But on reaching the summit, pause again, for westward views to Ben Vorlich and around are stunning, and to the south, Loch Lomond is there in all its glory. It is no wonder that photographers are captivated by it.

You will leave the Watershed here, for it continues north by some equally ragged hills including Stob nan Eighrach (613m), and crossing the head of Glen Gyle to Parlan Hill and Beinn Chabhair (933m) and so much else, beyond.

The Exit

Retrace to the Bealach a'Mheim, for what will then be a difficult descent to the Snaid Burn and Garrison. Going down is always more difficult in terms of route finding and safety, than going up. On an ascent, you can at least see in advance, where you might put your feet.

And so back to the car, and the feeling of a superb and probably unusual day out, in which the Watershed has provided a rewarding, if at times quite challenging experience.

Walk 11   Ben Lui and Her Neighbours
Sheet 50
Distance 27km (1 : 25 : 1) – 13 hours
Access by car and train, or bus

A great ark of very fine mountains that are a familiar site for all who journey north from Crianlarich, whether by car on the A82, by train on the West Highland Line, or indeed on foot and by bike on the West Highland Way. A look to the left on the way to Tyndrum, and a trio of great peaks cut a sharp profile on the skyline, and if they are in any way articulated with snow in the gullies, the scene is yet more appealing. That horizon is the Watershed, and most surely beckons, for those who wish to experience this particular grandeur.

If it is being tackled in a single day, it will be a long and strenuous one, will repay with all of the pleasures that following a ridge, or close succession of hills brings. The trio of Munros are normally climbed together either directly from Tyndrum and Cononish or Dalrigh, and it remains to be seen what, if any, the impact of recently approved resumption of mining for precious metals at Cononish will have on this.

The fine trio of Ben Lui (1,130m), Ben Oss (1,029m) and Beinn Dubhchraig (978m) take the elevation well past the thousand metre mark for the first time in this selection of Watershed walks.

Obstacles   3 fences, one railway, few sheep, and no beasts.

The Approach

Tyndrum is the starting point, and offers the options of getting there by car, train or bus. A path heads west from the rear

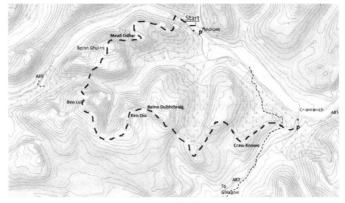

Route Map 11

of the hotel, and follows a route through woodland to the spoil heap remains of former lead mining activity. Join the Watershed near the bottom of this man-made scree, and a zigzag path will help with the ascent.

The Walk

To reach this point, the Watershed has come from Beinn Odhar (901m) with a relentlessly steep descent to the West Highland Way and railway crossing north of Tyndrum. It has then climbed onto the more modest Beinn Bheag (653m), and a leisurely descent through the forest to only the second house on or about Watershed on this, the Heartland March, beside the Oban road and railway crossings.

Climbing up out of the mining debris, and a right turn brings you up to *the soldier's nose*, on Sron nan Colan (590m). This is followed by Creag Bhuidhe *yellow craig –*

the soft yellow of dried grasses and bents, and colour of nature's palate features again with Meall Odhar (656m) *the dun or tawny heap or lump* (though the heap or lump part of it is a rather uncomplimentary). Beinn Chuirn (880m) *hill of the cairn* takes the route a good bit higher, with a scramble round the lip of Coire na Saobhaidhe – a reference to something foolish! Three wide sweeps to left and right and left again, above steep craigs include spot 773 The deep and steep valleys to the left are a great favourite for winter climbers. Ciochan Beinn Laoigh *little nipple of hill of the calf* provides a brief respite before the final assault on Ben Lui (1,130m *hill of the calf,* itself. Much of the area to the left up to this point is the Ben Lui National Nature reserve, and many years of woodland regeneration has helped to greatly enrich the habitat for wildlife. In addition to this designation, there is also an sssi, Special Area of Conservation, and much of it defined as a National Scenic Area. This is no ordinary mountain collection and associated landscape; it has status. A major secondary watershed meets our main Watershed at this point – that of the Clyde catchment and the very short River Awe, it's much longer loch and tributaries including the Lochy and the Orchy. Though it could well be argued, that since these in fact empty into Loch Etive well before the open sea, then the River Etive is in fact the primary river system. In any event, it is a very long watershed to Sron Uamha *cave of the nose, at* the point of the Mull of Kintrye which is nearest to Ireland. The author is very happy to leave it to someone else to tackle that one – and has doubts if the Kintrye Way would be of much help in such a venture.

The second Munro in this trio is Ben Oss (1,029m) *loch-*

outlet hill: a reference to the glacially created hollow below in which Loch Oss lies, I suspect. Much of the terrain underfoot on all of the higher ground is over rock and loose stones, of which it could at least be said 'sans bog'. Beinn Dubhchraig (978m) *black-rock hill* concludes the threesome, and there is a striking contrast between the line of craigs which fall away steeply to the right, and the less frantic slopes that slide down the Allt Coire Dubhchraig to the left. With a relatively steep descent of nigh-on 500m, the route then slopes more gently, though less firmly, to spot 588 where a sharp left turn then takes it towards the top of the forest area, but don't be misled as Creagan Soillear *conspicuous little cliff* is the real target. Swing round to the right to the next forest edge, and Craw Knowe – reference to a crow, and follow the fence to Kirk Craig and reach the West Highland Way where it enters the forest on the left. Leave the Watershed at this point.

Were you to continue on the Watershed, you would cross the A82 and the railway at the very head of Glen Falloch, and head for Cruach Ardrain (1,046m) and its neighbours, by way of the Grey Heights.

The Exit

At the forest edge on the West Highland Way, a path goes off to the left through the forest to Crianlarich. Resume whatever arrangements you have made to either pick up your car, or make use of public transport.

Walk 12   Corrour to Dalwhinnie
Sheets 41 and 42
Distance 51km (6 : 36 : 9) – 2 days
Access by train

This walk packs it in in terms of Watershed features. A fine weekend in the mountains, with what might be called 'train to train' at either end, and starting off at the station that is often accredited as *dropping you off in the middle of nowhere*. The route bounds one of the great private estates where conservation and biodiversity are being pursued with a passion, in partnership with one of our leading environmental charities, the John Muir Trust. Part of it includes an area with the double designation of sssi and Special Area of Conservation. There's the appeal of a night in a favourite remote hostel, and another in an ever popular bothy – though in both cases, camping is a worthy alternative. And the walk ventures as close as the Watershed gets to the geographic centre of Scotland, no less.

Many would acknowledge that at least one of the mountains that this walk includes has iconic status and gives a real sense of remoteness.

A quartet of great mountains dominates this outing, but they are accompanied by a number of equally fine, if rather smaller peaks, to make for a superb route and walk. Carn Dearg (941m), Sgor Gaibhre (955m), Ben Alder (1,148m) and Beinn Bheoil (1,019m) make up this foursome. This is followed by a stretch of low moor, and then a rarely climbed Beinn Eilde (674m) to the north east of Loch Pattack.

Obstacles   4 fences, few sheep and no beasts.

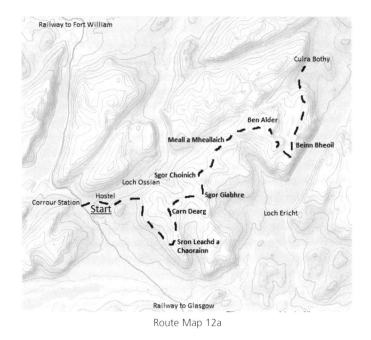

Route Map 12a

The Approach

Trains leave from Glasgow Queen Street, and there are three services each day (Mon – Sat) departing at 8.21, 12.21 and 18.21, and arriving at Corrour at 11.20, 15.20, and 21.19 respectively. There may be variations in these, according to winter and summer timetables, Sunday services, and any subsequent timetable alterations. There is currently only one form of hostel accommodation in the vicinity of Corrour Station, The Corrour Station restaurant has recently (2012)

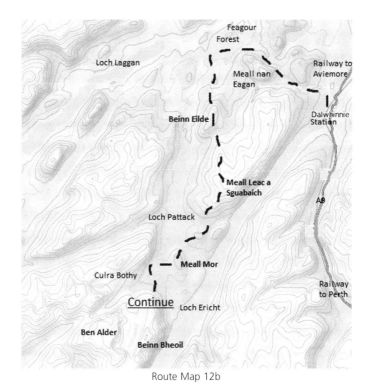

Route Map 12b

reopened. Loch Ossian Hostel is a Scottish Youth Hostels Association (SYHA) facility, located about a mile from the station (by track), is open April to October, and has been upgraded to a high eco-standard. Booking is strongly advised.

This walk is a relatively demanding two day venture, with time allowed at either end for rail travel. An early start on the first walking day is essential.

From the Corrour Station walk along the track to the Loch Ossian Hostel, and turn off the track onto a path to the right, which then continues east to Peter's Rock. The objective is Carn Dearg, and this can be reached most directly by climbing the shoulder of Meall na Leitire Dubh *lump of the black slope*, so called perhaps because its northern slopes do not receive any direct sunshine in the winter months. An easy short ridge leads along the lip of Corie Creagach *corrie of the craigs* on the left to Carn Dearg (941m) *red hill*, where you join the Watershed.

The Walk

To get to this point, the Watershed has come up a long ridge to the south, including Sron Leachd a'Chaorainn. This has been preceded by a 50km clockwise circumnavigation of Rannoch Moor from the head of the Water of Tulla. The whole area, and much of the route abounds in designated and protected sites; its landscapes and habitats are clearly of great importance. Much of 52,000 acre Corrour Estate lies to the left on the hills that encircle Loch Ossian. Acquired a number of years ago by a family that generated its wealth from the profits derived from milk packaging, it is gradually changing from being solely a sporting estate, to one in which biodiversity is now the prime goal. With support and advice from the John Muir Trust, it is combining the regeneration of native woodland and associated habitats, with reduction in deer numbers, and positively fostering public access. Sustainability is woven into this, and will it is anticipated create many lasting benefits to wildlife, and our enjoyment of it.

From Carn Dearg, the route heads north east by Mam Ban *female breast* to Sgor Gaibhre (955m) *goat's peak*. The terrain makes for fine walking on firm grasses, and once again, 'sans bog', and the steepish down's and ups seem somehow so much easier thereby. Small cairns mark each successive summit, and the *goat's peak* is a good place to stop and stare. Loch Ossian to the north, is enchanting, for not only is the loch itself a thing of great beauty, but the name has so many romantic associations. But whether Ossian ever came to these parts is a matter of conjecture, so best to leave it at that, for fear of demystifying the place. Across the Loch is a top which is a great favourite for either Munro completions, or a quick ascent between the times of the first and last train of the day – Beinn na Lap (935m) is a popular mountain. To the south lies the erstwhile Rannoch Forest; with not a native tree in sight, but some pretty extensive areas of deep peat bog and hag, which from up on these heights, look quite uncrossable. Loch Ericht stretches away to the north east, with a hint of the southern Cairngorms beyond. And to the west, that great massif of Aonach Beag and the line of mountains beyond Loch Treig, somehow grouped together on the map as Killiechonate Forest.

The *pass of the sharp steep hill* Bealach nan Sgor is followed by the very hill, Sgor Choinnich (929m) – not quite a Munro, but a superb hill none the less. Meall a'Bhealaich (865m) – *lump of the pass,* where the top is covered with boulders and gritty sand. This succession of tops concludes with Beinn a'Chumhainn (903m), before a steep drop into the Bealach Cumhann or *narrow pass;* a very apt description. The ascent onto the Ben Alder plateau is by a relentless steep 400m climb, or should it be scramble, with the Bealach Dubh or *black pass* round to the left, and on the right more of those 'rocky doodles' by way of a rough wall of rock dropping almost sheer into the Bealach Cumhann on its way to the haunted Benalder Cottage and the shores of Loch Ericht.

This formidable ascent barely prepares you for the contrasting character of the Ben Alder plateau: half a square kilometre of very gently sloping grasslands and small rocks high on a mountain top. The summit cairn is a great rough collection of these stones, with a pile here, and a sort of crude circular shelter there. The meaning of Ben Alder is obscure, but may be the *hill of the rock water*, but mystery aside, it is a vantage point par-excellence; time to admire and contemplate.

One question that has challenged generations of people living here in Scotland is where is the centre, or heart, of the country? Where is the point that is furthest from the sea in every direction? Various methods have been used to provide a satisfactory answer, and not least amongst them was the low-tech combination of a map of the country, a pin and a bit of string. This came up with various solutions and hence locations. More recently, the OS employed a high-tech method, and a visit to Wikepedia on the subject will tell you all about the method and the conclusion. I have chosen to call this whole section of the Watershed the Heartland March – from the Highland Boundary Fault to the Great Glen, because it does indeed take the Watershed close to the heart of Scotland. The NN ten-point reference for this is unnecessary here, but I will say that it is 14.5km east of Beinn Bheoul, on the eastern shoulder of Sron na h-Eiteich, 300m from the railway and the A9, and just less than 2.5km from Dalnaspidal Lodge. So now you know.

I invite you at this stage to get out a map of the Central Highlands of Scotland, and pore over the features, specific tops, mountain ranges, lochs, and the entire panorama that can be experienced from the top of Ben Alder; it is outstanding. And I invite you, if you are reasonably fit, to be sure and include this one in your Watershed walks. If the weather is clear, you will be rewarded tenfold.

The descent, past Sron Bealach Beithe to Bealach Breabag *pass of the little height* needs some care, and it is best to err to the south and onto firmer terrain. It is strange that spot 955 appears to be un-named on the map, for whatever name it does have, it will surely denote something impressive, if for no other reason than it gives excellent views both ways on Loch Ericht. But there is a clue in the name of the adjacent corrie: Sron Coire na h-Iolaire (955m) *nose of the eagle's corrie*. That will do nicely. There is remarkably little vegetation on Beinn Bheoil (1,019m) *hill of the mouth*, a great whale-back of rock, giving almost a kilometre of the finest walking. Bealach Beithe *pass of the birch*, with its loch of the same name lies at an elevation of just over 700m, below the scree-slope to the left, whilst Loch Ericht lies almost 700m below this summit. This landscape gives a real impression of size, with almost everything about it being on a grand scale: the human presence is so small.

We are nearing journey's end, for the day at least. To the north, Loch Pattack catches the late light, and a couple of kilometres this side of it are two diminutive buildings; the one on the right is Culra Bothy, and hopefully some space in it will be available for your sleeping bag and mat. So continue right along the ridge, past another Sron, and then dropping down to the north west to pick up the path, which is not only pretty much on the Watershed as it nears the river, and leads to the bridge across to the bothy. With three rooms, and a stove in one of them, it is a fine bothy, and you will benefit if some other occupants have brought some coal for the stove. There might just be some good craic round a cheery fire, with a mug of something fitting in your fist.

Day two will be less demanding, though it will involve some bog-hopping perhaps. Back across the bridge, and onto the ignominiously named *big lump*, or Meall Mor (528m), and as you make your way to Meall Beag (518m) *little lump*, you might well be struck with how this almost featureless moor (bog) contrasts with yesterday's terrain. The sandy shores of Loch Pattack do look inviting though. Cross the track ahead and there should be a clearing in the forest to take you up the shoulder to the right of Coire na Longairt and onto Meall Leac na Sguabaich – a reference to a lump with a big flat stone. Continue north by spot 528 to Beinn Eilde (674m) *hill abounding in hinds*, which gives a bit of respite to what is otherwise a boggy and tussock-ridden section – but that is wildness for you, and in season it will have all of its share of wild flowers. You might even hear the mocking call of the cuckoo to cheer you on your way. Bear left of the Dark Gully, and ponder how you will deal with the formidable deer fence that lies ahead at the edge of the forest. The gate to the left near the Falls of Pattack may be the answer, but once into the forest, do re-join the Watershed and take a bearing for the site of the pre-clearance village in the clearing. At this point you will leave the Watershed.

Were you to stay on it, the route goes frustratingly north east to the end of the culvert that takes the waters of the River Mashie to join the River Pattack just west of Feagour.

This is following a difficult slog through the forest to Creag Ruadh (560m) and onwards to Carn Liath and Stop Poite Coire Ardair, to round the head of the Spey – see walk 14.

The Exit

There is a train to be caught! So follow the right angle in the forest track and head south west on the path which leads to Dalwhinnie. There are four trains a day (Mon – Sat) that stop at Dalwhinnie heading south, as follows: 10.30, 15.54 and 21.28 to Glasgow, and 19.58 to Edinburgh. Sunday services are: 13.46 to Glasgow, and 19.39 to Edinburgh (correct at time of printing). All services go via Perth, which increases the options further south.

Walk 13   Ossian and Alder
Sheets 41 and 42
Distance 34km (8 : 13 : 13) – 13hrs
Access by train

Thoughts of Loch Ossian and Ben Alder are evocative for all lovers of wild places; its remoteness conjures such appealing images of mountain and loch, which are far, far removed from contemporary urban life. And there is romantic association, for Oisin was the son of that great character from Irish mythology, Fionn mac Cumhaill. He was alleged to be the narrator, or indeed the author of a cycle of poems, which have come down to us through the Scottish collector James Macpherson. Ossian has clearly had a wide impact on lore and legend, for in Scotland alone, in addition to this very fine loch, he also has a cave, grave, and even a Hall named after him. We are touched by these romantic dreamings, so where better to start a very fine day walk in which our spirits will soar; we will be uplifted.

Carn Dearg (941m), Sgor Gaibhre (955m) and Ben Alder (1,148m) combine with a number of other neighbouring hills, and some distinctive Bealachs to give a route that is never dull.

Obstacles   1 fence, few sheep, and no beasts.

The Approach

This is the same approach as for the previous weekend walk, and the author recommends the overnight beforehand whether in hostel or tent, it will help promote that real sense of anticipation which it fully merits. A variation would be

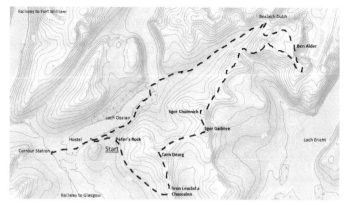

Route Map 13

to walk past Peter's Rock and the remains of Corrour Old Lodge, as far as the County Boundary, and turn up and left onto Sron Leachd a Chaorainn. At this point you will join the Watershed, which has crossed the low ground to the west, and the railway, from A Chruach on the north side of Rannoch Moor.

The Walk

From Sron Leachd a'Chorainn, the walk is north to Carn Dearg, with perhaps a reference to an eagle's nest on the right with Creag na h-lolaire. The journey then follows the same route as the previous walk, but only as far as either the Bealach Cumhann, or Ben Alder. If you choose the latter, then be prepared for a challenging descent on the north side of the mountain to the Bealach Dubh, or an additional 10km round by the Allt a Bhealaich Bheithe.

The Exit

In any event, from the head of the Bealach Cumhann, return to Loch Ossian by the Uisge Labhair, the *speaking water*. The track along the south side of the loch is little used by estate vehicles, and is the quieter for that. It also goes through some of the now mature woodland planted by Sir John Stirling Maxwell a hundred or more years ago.

Trains from Corrour to Glasgow are at 08.30, 12.41 and 18.25 (correct at time of printing).

Walk 14   Round the Headwaters of the Spey
Sheets 35 and 34
Distance 36km (5 : 18 : 13) – 13hrs
Access by car

The River Spey is without doubt one of Scotland's iconic rivers, and most people are familiar with some part of it, be it around Loch Insch and Aviemore for the outdoor experience in that wider area, or further downstream with its whisky trail fame. But the upper reaches are less well known and a little off the beaten track, where some of the River's waters are 'pochled' to flow west by Loch Laggan for hydro power. A walk on the hills and mountains round the headwaters, and in sight of Loch Spey has so much to offer – fine views and a great sense of place, landscape evolution and a touch of history too.

Somewhat in the shadow of its more popular neighbours, Carn Liath (1,006m), is then followed by Stob Poite Coire Ardair 1,051m), and Creag a'Bhanain (849m). Carn Leac (884m) then marks the drop into the Corrieyairack Pass.

Obstacles   2 fences, no sheep, and no beasts.

The Approach

Drive west along the U road from Laggan and the A86 from Newtonmore, and park at Garva Bridge. Walk and climb south to pick up the National Park boundary by Stac Buidhe *yellow steep hill* and Carn Dubh *black hill* to join the Watershed at Spot 916 above Coire Dubh *black corrie*.

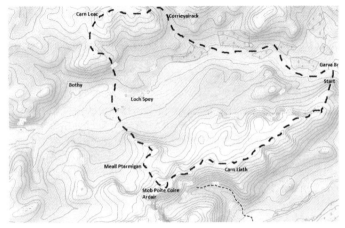

Route Map 14

The Walk

To get to this point, the Watershed has crossed by Meall Ghoirleig and Glen Shirra from Meall a t-Sithcin and Feagour.

The ridge of A'Bhuidheanach *yellow place* leads up to Carn Liath (1,006m) *grey hill*, with a gradual ascent and exceptionally fine walking on a landscape of rocks and grass. This is approaching the edge of the Creag Meagaidh National Nature Reserve. A break in the walking to take in the views will indeed be rewarding. To the east lie the southern Cairngorms, stretching beyond Glenfeshie Forest to Cairn Toul and its neighbours. Tree rimmed Loch Laggan to the south catches the light against the darker outlines of Beinn a'Chlachair and Aonach Beag beyond Ardverikie. The great craigs and corries of Creag Meagaidh dominate the view to the west. A rather diminutive Loch Spey to the north suggests the start of that famous river, and beyond that, the Corrieyairack Pass disappears into the hills around the further extremities of today's venture.

A series of three minor summits start with Meall an t-Snaim (969m), Spot 963, and Sron Coire a Chriochairean (991m) *reference to a boundary* conclude with Stob Poite Coire Ardair (north top 1,051m) *peak of the pot of the high corrie*. This is a precious landscape, and much of this is recognised in the quadruple designations of SSSI, Special Protection Area, Special Area of Conservation and of course the National Nature Reserve. Mountain enthusiasts might wish to continue round to the left to take in the full wonders of the mountains above the Coire Ardair, but that appealing temptation must be supressed for now, because our particular Ribbon of Wildness heads northwards by a steady descent to Meall Ptarmigan (815m) *lump or hill of the ptarmigan* and the ridge to Creag a'Mhanain. A further ridge running to the north-west takes us to the definitive Sron Nead *nose of the nest*. Beyond, lies 2km of bog and moss, with the puny remains of a fence slowly disappearing into the watery vegetation. But before picking a route off the end of the nose, do look left to the upper reaches of Glen Roy with its parallel roads, created variously by Fionn mac Cumhaill or glacial retreat.

Before the glaciers retreated and the levels of the lochs that they held back left these 'shorelines', the watershed was confused, with water spilling across the col and into what we now call the Spey. Luib-chonnal *settlement at the bend* bothy lies to the left of the young forest on the slopes beyond the col. Firmer and steeper ground is reached with the ascent onto Creag a'Chail (760m) and Carn Leac (884m) *hill of the bare or large rock*, where we leave the Watershed. It heads west by Poll-gormack Hill and Carn Dearg before dropping into the chasm of the Great Glen.

The Exit

Descend to the north east by Spot 879 to reach General Wade's Military Road in the Corrieyairack Pass. This will bring you back to your vehicle at Garva Bridge by way of the famous hairpin bends, and Melgarve. The route is only marred by the line of pylons and cables overhead – part of the Beauly to Denny upgrade, it is to be regretted.

Walk 15 – Above the Parallel Roads of Roy
   Sheet 34
   Distance 27km (8 : 13 : 6) – 11hrs
   Access by car

Many people come and marvel at Glen Roy's configuration of 'parallel roads'. Although the formal explanation for what created these three level terraces, one below the other on much of the hillsides in the glen, is that a glacier in Great Glen held back large bodies of water in the glens to the east, history has had its more fanciful and romantic theories – not least amongst them, the activities of sundry giants. Either way, these shoreline terraces are impressive. They most certainly tend to eclipse the fact that the Watershed lies above the head-waters of both Glen Roy and its feeder, Glen Turret. But today's outing will address this popular error, and celebrate the ribbon of wildness on the map hereabouts.

A rewarding walk awaits those who will venture beyond the popular appeal of Glen Roy though; wildness abounds, views are impressive, and a sense of remoteness beckons.

Carn Leac (884m), Pol-gormack Hill (806m) and Carn Dearg (815m) represent some of the higher points on this walk, which also includes more than one stretch of notable peat hag. Perhaps the emerging views of the Great Glen offer a stunning piece of compensation though.

Obstacles   3 fences, few sheep and no beasts.

The Approach

Drive up Glen Roy from the A86 at Roy Bridge, to the end of the public road at Brae Roy Lodge. Walk up the valley to

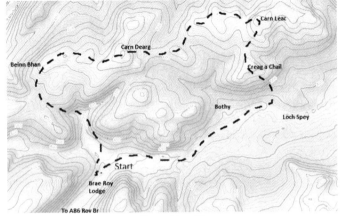

Route Map 15

the north and east, staying on the left side of the river. The track will eventually become a path, as it passes Luib-chonnal *the settlement at the bend* bothy. The river crossing just beyond the bothy can be difficult, so care may be needed, especially if you wish to remain dry-shod. Join the Watershed at the coll.

The Walk

The Watershed has reached this point by way of a bog crossing from Sron Nead and the lesser top of Stob Poite Coire Ardair. Turn left onto firmer ground and the ascent of Creag a'Chail (760m) and Carn Leac (884m), where the Corrieyairack Pass with its famous Military Road created in the 18th Century by General Wade, opens out to the right. The line of pylons, which form part of the infamous Beauly to Denny upgrade, add nothing to the landscape; they are a blot on it.

So turn your back on the blight, and head for Poll-gormack Hill (806m) via spot 778, and then fix your sights on Leac nan Uan (693m). An area of severe peat hag separates you from that modest hill though, and you will be intrigued at the remains of a disintegrating fence that somehow crosses these hags. A steady ascent onto Carn Dearg (815m) *red hill* will quickly banish all memories of peat, for now at least, as the long gradual descent to Carn na Larach (745m) takes over. This has a strange name, for it can variously mean the hill with the site of a building or ruin, a battlefield, scar or impression. Beinn Bhan (712m) is more straightforward though, as it is simply the *female hill*. The drama of the Great Glen will be at your feet here. The entire length of Loch Lochy draws the eye to the south west, with forest on the slopes of both sides and higher mountains which carry the Watershed, forming the right hand skyline. Ben Tee (Walk 16) stands bold and fine straight across the Glen, and to the north east, Loch Oich, and then at least the start of Loch Ness marks almost half of this 700m deep trench running across Scotland.

The Exit

The Descent will be fairly steep in places, so it is suggested that the best route is as follows. To Teanga Bheag *the little tongue* cross higher up the Allt Teanga Bige, and go to the north western end of Meall a Chomhlain, continue south west to the col at spot 357. Follow the northern side of the Allt a Chomhlain into Glen Turret, crossing the River Turret by the bridge and picking up the track which then goes to Brae Roy Lodge and transport home after a good and varied hill-day.

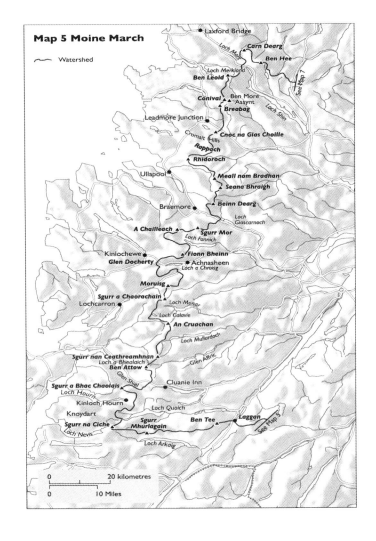

Map 5 Moine March

⌒ Watershed

Laxford Bridge
Loch More
Carn Dearg
Ben Hee
See Map 7
Loch Merkland
Ben Leold
Ben More
Assynt
Conival
Breabag
Loch Shin
Leadmore Junction
Cromalt Hills
Cnoc na Glas Choille
Rappoch
Rhidoroch
Ullapool
Meall nam Bradhan
Seana Bhraigh
Braemore
Beinn Dearg
Loch Glascarnoch
A Chailleach
Sgurr Mor
Loch Fannich
Kinlochewe
Fionn Bheinn
Glen Docherty
Achnasheen
Loch a Chroisg
Moruisg
Sgurr a Chaorachain
Lochcarron
Loch Monar
Loch Calavie
An Cruachan
Loch Mullardoch
Sgurr nan Ceathreamhnan
Loch a Bhealaich
Glen Affric
Ben Attow
Glen Shiel
Sgurr a Bhac Chaolais
Cluanie Inn
Loch Hourn
Kinloch Hourn
Loch Quoich
Ben Tee
Laggan
Knoydart
Sgurr na Ciche
Sgurr Mhurlagain
See Map 5
Loch Nevis
Loch Arkaig

0   20 kilometres

0   10 Miles

The Moine March (6)

MOINE, AT OVER 330km is the longest of the five Marches on the Watershed of Scotland, and its average elevation of some 595m ensures that her head is often in the clouds. The 25 Munros and 13 Corbetts add an enervating emphasis to the fine high roll-call in a very topical way, and the 23 designated and protected areas that straddle or flank this part of the Watershed will help significantly to focus on both the evidence and picture of wildness along the way. Almost entirely devoid of house or barn throughout, and the grand total of only eight public road crossings in this long meander, merely serves to punctuate the emptiness.

But bald statistics provide only part of the picture. Starting at Laggan in that trench, the Great Glen, which slices bold and straight right across Scotland, the Moine March then, takes a vast sweep west to Sgurr na Ciche in the Rough Bounds. This proximity to the west coast is maintained throughout, and in a number of places her early morning shadows only slowly withdraw from the heads of the sea lochs. The word 'moine' has dual significance, for the Watershed here rides in tandem with that major geological feature, the Moine Thrust, and the word itself means a *bog* or *morass*, of which there are more than a few. It ends on Ben Hee, where rock and craig give way to the softer hues of the Flow Country.

Many of the landscapes that are dominated by or embrace the Watershed are of course iconic and hereabouts read like a litany of the best: the Rough Bounds, Glen Shiel, Kintail, West Monar, the Fannichs, Beinn Dearg and Seana Bhraigh,

Assynt, and many more; all combine to help define the qualities of the Moine March. It is explored in much greater detail in Ribbon of Wildness, but this selection of five walks will give a tantalising flavour of all that that this section of the Watershed has to offer.

Walk 16   The Fairy Hill
Sheet 34
Distance 23km (2 : 11 : 10) – 11hrs
Access by car or bus

The Great Glen is indeed 'great' in both name and character; an immense straight trough running across Scotland from Loch Linnhe to the Moray Firth. Substantially formed over 400 million years ago with a split in the evolving landform of what we now call Scotland, the land to the north moved south west by over 100km, relative to the rest of our land-mass. This split and movement in turn created a line of weakness, which was much more prone to erosion than that surrounding it; glacial activity then exploited this to the full.

The Watershed is crossed by The Great Glen just north of Laggan, *little hollow or dimple* and the Caledonian Canal, that links the three lochs in the Glen, and thence to salt water at either end.

Just two, but very dramatic mountains in this outing – Ben Tee (901m) and Meall a'Choire Ghlais (900m). Anything that this day may lack numerically, is more than compensated for by the quality and grandeur of these two mountains, and their wider setting.

Obstacles   2 fences, few sheep and no beasts.

The Approach

Travel on the A82, Fort William to Inverness to Laggan, just north of Loch Lochy, and park, by arrangement, at or about the Great Glen Hostel. Walk a short distance north to a point of access to the Great Glen Way, on your left. This follows the embankment for the Caledonian Canal to the Laggan Swing Bridge. Cross, and pick up the U road on the opposite side of the canal, and head south to join the Watershed at spot 41 just before Balma Glaster.

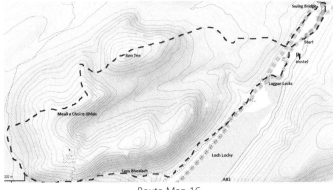

Route Map 16

The Walk

To reach this point, the Watershed has crossed the Great Glen from Beinn Bhan above the forest and Carn Dearg (see Walk 15), to the east.

On the steepish ascent to rise just south of Lochan Diota, there are very scattered remnants of juniper woodland – a native tree, and a few rhododendrons – an invasive species. Climb to the west by way of the ridge to the north of Coire Buidhe *yellow corrie* to reach the summit of Ben Tee (901m) *fairy hill*. This is a hill with four very different elevations. Its south face is a 300m run of scree, whilst to the north an arc of crags drops steeply. The steady ridge that you have just ascended from the east is in contrast to the steep, but thankfully firm descent that awaits, to the west.

If plans to build a massive pump-storage reservoir in this area come to fruition, it will forever change the view from, and the sense of remoteness on and about, these tops. The wildness of the Watershed will be severely compromised. The proposal is to construct an immense dam across the upper reaches of the Allt a Choire Ghlais, and thus create the upper reservoir, with Loch Lochy over 500m below forming the lower one. Even if all of the generating machinery is housed in a cavern carved out of the heart of the mountain, the impact of this upper sheet of water and it's shoreline scar will be destructive to an otherwise almost pristine landscape. This proposal is utterly misguided, and should be opposed by all who value Scotland's wild places.

The long level ridge of Meall a Choire Ghlais (900m) *lump of the grey/green corrie* is the next target, but not before a rapid 360m descent immediately followed by a similar ascent. The craigs present a challenge but there is a grassy avenue between them.

Extensive scree marks out the south side of this ridge that give such a pleasing high level walk. Then deep corries on either side cut into and narrow it, as it curves round to the south. The northern of these corries has the evocative name of Coire an Eich *corrie of the horse or brute*, whilst its southern counterpart is Coire Glas *grey/green corrie*. The descent towards Lochan Phudair in the Bealach to the west is an unrelenting 470m plunge. But the terrain is firm. You leave the Watershed on the track at 204953.

The westward sweep of the Watershed continues all the way to Sgurr na Ciche, in the Rough Bounds.

The Exit

A left turn on the path, which has come south from Glen Garry, takes you round to the east below the craigs of Sron a'Choire Ghairbh to the Cam Bhealach the *crooked or bent pass* before dropping into the forest and picking up the Great Glen Way. Cross the Caledonian Canal by Laggan Locks at the Ceann Loch bay of Loch Lochy. Follow the embankment back to the exit onto the A82 once more, and turn right to return to Great Glen Hostel.

Walk 17   The Upper Glen Quoich Round
Sheet 33
Distance 27km (5 : 15 : 7) – 12hrs
Access by car

The road to Kinlochhourn, one of the longest dead-ends in the entire country provides a view of extensive wildness; visually it is as near as any car can be driven to the area labelled Rough Bounds, it is truly an out of the way kind of place. Whilst the creation of the current Loch Quoich has dramatically changed the landscape in the valley bottom, the road has been re-routed to accommodate it, and a line of pylons marches defiantly. No doubt, if these man-made blemishes were being proposed today, the clamour against would be long and loud; the protest would be vociferous. But look beyond, and go beyond the immediate impact, and the mountains are as rough and rugged as nature made them.

So this walk exploits the access that the road does give to some exquisite wildness, and promises dramatic scenery. Sgurr a'Mhaoraich Beag (948m) sets the scene for the Watershed part of this day, which then goes on to include much of the western end of the much loved South Glen Shiel Ridge.

The Approach

Drive along the U road from the A87 as it passes by Loch Garry. Travel past Tomdoun, Kingie, and much of Loch Quoich. You should park beside the bridge at 015041, around spot 207. Walk half a kilometre further along the road, and turn right up the path by Bac nan Canaichean – a steady and demanding 680m ascent leading to Sgurr Coire nan Eirichealach (891m). A fine ridge walk, and another 136m of ascent then leads onto Sgurr a'Mhaoraich (1,027m). This top, although the higher of the Mhaoraichs is not on the Watershed, but on dropping to the smaller, Sgurr a Mhaoraich Beag (948m), the ribbon of wildness is reached.

Obstacles   2 fences, few sheep, and some beasts on the lower ground.

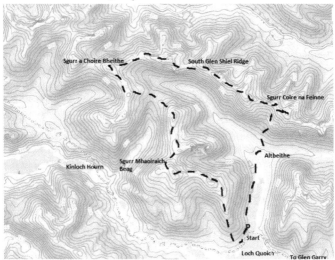

Route Map 17

The Walk

Savour this place, for the word spectacular somehow seems inadequate. Loch Hourn, our most fiord-like of sea lochs meanders westward, hemmed in by Knoydart on its south shores, and the base of Druim Fada on the other. The Sound of Sleat and Skye lie somewhere beyond. The mountains of Barrisdale largely obscure much of Knoydart, but these are the Rough Bounds, and the name is entirely apt; the description a perfect fit. To the south, the profile of the horizon is like a storm-tossed sea, with one crest of a wave after another. But this is rock, not water. Sgurr Mor and Gairich are perhaps the more familiar names, and beyond lies Glen Kingie, with another maelstrom of high rock beyond that. Eastwards, and Loch Garry points a tantalising way to the Great Glen somewhere beyond the forests. The unfamiliar back view of Glen Shiel ridge to the north is like a vast bastion.

Sgurr Thionail (906m) beckons to the north, and a rocky high-way is the route to get there. Wester Glen Quoich opens up at your feet, a 700m deep chasm. The back-side of Glen Shiel ridge is breath-taking – a 15 kilometre long succession of fine mountains (although there is in fact another six or more kilometres of it lying beyond the Bealach Duibh Leac at the head of this glen.

The rocky descent to Loch Bealach Coire Sgoireadail requires extreme care, and picking the Watershed amongst the craigs is not straightforward. With Sgurr a'Bhac Chaolais (885m) as the next goal, there is a steady climb, one in which the valley to the right seems to narrow and close-in. Coire Reidh on the left is one of those immense amphitheatres in the mountains, where some feature, in this case the ridge coming off Sgurr na Sgine gives extra emphasis to the scale and grandeur of the scene. But at Sgurr a'Bhac Chaolais, the route is a very sharp right turn round the head of the glen by the 720m high Bealach Duibh Leac, and a fine walk onto Creag nan Damh (918m), on the Glen Shiel Ridge, no less.

There are now two options: the first is to drop into

Wester Glen Quoich from the col before Sgurr Beag, and the alternative is to continue on the Watershed to Sgurr Coire na Feinne. So The Exit from this walk offers choice and opportunity.

If the former is chosen, the path is relatively easy to find, and descends to the path running along the floor of the Glen, on the north side of the Burn. This path should then be followed downstream to Alltbeithe, where a right turn will take you onto the estate track back to the bridge at spot 207.

If the latter course is chosen, it will add four tops to the walk, and a minor addition to the distance to be covered. Glen Shiel Ridge, in this case, the western end of it is undoubtedly one of the top ten or so such ridges in Scotland, in terms of popularity, access, and exhilaration. That this should be on the Watershed is all the better, as it thus forms part of the much more extensive route, and links it by yet more wildness to many other exquisite parts of the country; it is an integral part of the ribbon of wildness. Sgurr Beag (896m) comes next on the ridge, and it is to be lamented that a path bypasses its top, for those who dismiss it simply because it is not a Munro. Shocking! Sgurr an Lochain (1,004m) continues this litany of excellence, and illustrates to perfection, the contrast between the north and south sides of this ridge. The north is deeply cut and sculpted by corries, and rough ridges stretch out before dropping steeply into the glen. The south face of the ridge is significantly less rocky, and with only a few outcrops, presents an altogether smoother profile, articulated by short steep straight burns that make their hasty journey to the join the Wester Glen Quoich burn far below.

The walk onto Sgurr an Doire Leathain (1,010m) is a delight, for the ridge continues sharp and clear, and indeed, almost straight. Finally, Sgurr Coire na Feinne (902m) con-cludes the Watershed section of this great ridge. To descend, return to the col some 400m north west of the top, and drop to meet the path close to the Teanga na Feinne, which will bring you down to the path in the bottom of the Glen, referred to earlier. This in turn leads past Alltbeithe, and onto the estate track back to the bridge at spot 207.

Walk 18   A High Point and the Mountain with Two Names

Sheet 33
Distance 37km (15 : 18 : 4) – 18 hrs
Access by car or bus

A stop at the Cluanie Inn on the A87 road to Skye is as good a place as any to ponder and appreciate great mountain surroundings - from the comfort of a hostelry. There are of course other contenders for this; Kingshouse, Clachaig, Sligachan, Kinlochewe, and so on, the names are legendary. But whatever the particular merits or superlatives of each, Cluanie Inn is in a truly impressive location. To the south, lies an immense area of mountain and loch, which is barely scratched by the two very long and lonely dead-end roads that struggle through. Whilst to the north is an even greater road-less area – Achnasheen is almost 50km away, as the eagle might fly, or glide.

This area can boast the highest point on the entire Watershed at 1,143m, the mountain with two names, the crossing of one of the favourite coast to coasts, a delightful and very remote hostel, and so much more. Although the approach to the Watershed is lengthy, it will repay the effort many times over.

It may be a longish walk-in but Sgurr nan Ceathreamhnan (1,143m top) is the trophy, followed closely by Beinn Fhada (1,032m), and the whole, rounded off with Sgurr a'Bhealaich Dheirg (1,036m). Mountains with attitude.

Obstacles   3 fences, few sheep, and no beasts.

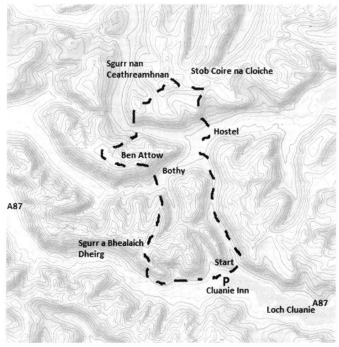

Route Map 18

The Approach

Travel on the A87 to the Cluanie Inn and park. Walk east to pick up the start of the track heading north through An Caorann Mor to the head of Glen Affric. There is a choice of accommodation; either Camban Bothy 2km to the south west in Fionngleann, or Alltbeithe Hostel (advance booking advised), 1km to the east. The route continues north by the path onto Stob Coire na Cloiche, and then west along the ridge by spots 941 and 970 to the higher of the tops of Sgurr nan Ceathreamhnan (1,151m), the Watershed is reached at the lower top of this very fine hill at 1,143m.

The Walk

The Watershed would continue north of here passing right through one of the biggest almost uninhabited areas in the country. Stuc Mor, An Cruachan, Beinn Dronaig, Beinn Tharsuinn, Sgurr Choinnich, Sgurr a'Chaorachain, and so many more magnificent mountains, guide or bear the Watershed through unforgettable landscapes. But that is for another day.

Our route takes us south and then west by spot 910 and Sgurr Gaorsaic (839m), before the descent to the track crossing from Glen Affric to Loch a'Bhealaich, and Morvich.

Ben Attow or Beinn Fhadda *the long mountain* is the next target, just to the south west, and access is by way of a challenging 600m ascent of a sharp spur with Coire Toll a'Mhadaidh to the left. The summit of Ben Attow (1,032m) should not be hurried; the panoramas in every direction must be savoured, with each mountain top and glen to be identified. East lies Glen Affric with its loch of the same name fringed by regenerating native forest. To the north, that vast empty area already referred to, almost devoid of habitation, spreads out in an immense patchwork of loch and hill, with glens pointing this way and that; it has a complex and enticing landform. Whilst to the west, the area of Kintail is punctuated by the Five Sisters' in a profile and texture that is truly breath-taking. Beyond, lies Loch Duich pointing its crooked finger towards Skye.

The name Ben Attow is so fitting, for the summit alone is some 3.5km long, and so we venture to its eastern extremity at Sgurr a'Dubh Doire (962m). The descent to Cnoc Biodaig (361m) in Fionngleann is demanding, but on firm grassy terrain. An area of native trees planted by the National Trust for Scotland must be skirted, or a robust deer fence scaled – twice. The way to Sgurr a'Bhealaich Dheirg some 3km to the south is upwards with well over 600m of fine clear ridge of Sreath a Ghlas-choire. The Allt a'Ghlas-choire, with its glacier scoured lochan at the foot of the craigs is on the right, and Coire nan Eun on the left. As you reach the summit of Sgurr a'Bhealaich Dheirg (1,036m), a new panorama and distant horizon spreads wide before you; from one wildness to the next, and beyond.

The ridge curves briefly to the left round the head of Coire nan Eun, but you must follow the Watershed south on a spur to Spot 806, followed by Meall a'Charra and a by way of a gap in the cleared forest to the A87 west of spot 271.

The Exit

Rather than return to the Cluanie Inn by walking along the road, pick up either the forest track or Old Military Road before dropping right down to the A87, and thus avoid having to walk alongside a lot of disconcerting and impatient traffic.

Walk 19   The Glen Carron Experience
Sheet 25
Distance 45km (7.5 : 28.5 : 9) – 22hrs
Access by car

For those who seek a novel purpose in heading for the hills or mountains, the Watershed does offer something entirely original. Although a great many have walked and climbed bits of it, probably whilst engaged on some other venture, a mere handful have walked it in its entirety – or their versions of it, at least. It has been immensely gratifying to see how quickly people warm to the very concept of the Watershed; how readily they pick up on its key place in the Scottish landform and landscapes, when they read or hear about it. And most quickly grasp the notion of largely continuous wildness too; the evidence and importance of this is compelling. So providing a brief guide to a number of discreet and achievable sections of the Watershed, will perhaps prove to be helpful, not least because it will answer the problem of how to tackle bits of what is essentially a linear route, without ending up some distance from transport at the end of each outing.

This need has called for a bit of inventiveness, and it could be that some of the walks do look either improbable or even imaginative, depending upon the reader or walker's knowledge of the Scottish countryside. The Watershed is the constant in all of this though, and it is not placed where it is for our convenience particularly; we need to work to its demands and immense opportunities; it is nature's gift.

The hills around Glen Carron provide both variety and delight; quality walking and more than just a hint of remoteness. The meanderings of the Watershed offer here a particular two day outing with wild camping to give that added pleasure and closeness to nature.

The more rounded hills to the north of the A890 including Beinn na Feusaige (625m) soon give way to a clutch of very striking tops, including Moruisg (928m), Sgurr a'Chaorachain (1,053m) and Beinn Tharsuinn (863m). This giant roller coaster of a route is cut by a number of deep and steep bealachs to set the heart racing.

Obstacles   5 fences, 1 railway, few sheep, and no beasts.

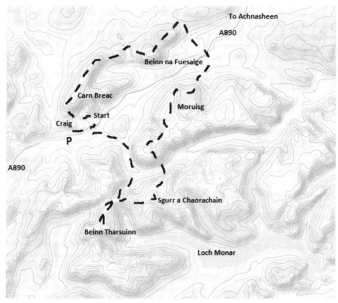

Route Map 19

The Approach

Travel on the A890 to Craig, 4km north east of Achnashellach, and park in one of the suitable areas beside the road. Walk north-east on the road for 1.5km to the start of the forest track on the left at 054503. Follow this track, which then becomes a path to the point where it emerges onto more open hill. Take a bearing for the point where the deer fence crosses the upper reaches of the Allt Dearg. You will find a clever device for keeping deer out, as the fence crosses the burn; this can be raised without much difficulty, even in winter conditions, and you will be able to pass underneath. You are now aiming for Carn Breac (678m), and have a choice of routes, both of which will be quite steep, but on open ground. Either follow the fence to the right and onto the shoulder to the right of Coire an Uilt Dheirg, and then north before swinging west onto the main ridge leading up to Carn Breac. Or alternatively follow the fence to the left and directly onto the steeper slopes which then become the main ridge. Continue north-east, to join the Watershed at 052538.

The Walk

To reach this point the Watershed has come south from Bidein Clann Raonaild by way of Carn Loisgt and Cul Leathaid, skirting the edges of the Moine Mhor *big morass*. Turn east to Meallan Mhic Iamhair (499m), and round the north side Loch of the same name, where the going will be soft. Head onto firmer ground for Beinn na Feusaige (625m), south of Lochan Sgeireach and onwards to Carn Beag (550m) with its trig point. Then drop steeply to the south, and round the lochan beside the Mile Dubh. The going will once again be soft, and there may be areas of open water to be navigated round. Spot 197 on the A890 is the target, where two strange standing stones on the north side suggest some ancient monument. Note the word, suggest.

Cross the road and the railway, and head south west for Cnoc na Moine (600m). A pronounced spur from Moruisg *big water* marks out an imminent 400m ascent rounding the Coire na Glas-lic, with its corrie loch below. And no sooner on the summit of Moruisg (928m), than the steep craggy exposure shifts to the right, around the Corie Toll nam Bian. The ridge is a delight to walk on though, gently sloping down to spot 854 on smooth firm terrain. Sgurr nan Ceannaichean (915m) *peak of the merchants or pedlars* is one of a few tops on the Watershed that requires a bit of interpretation as to whether it is indeed on the Watershed. Rounding the lip of the Coire an Tuill Bhain to the summit is clear enough, but a couple of small burns draining from half way down the southern slopes confuse the picture somewhat. By descending the shoulder running south east to the track crossing in the valley below, it is the author's interpretation that the summit is in fact just on the Watershed.

The ascent to the Sron na Frianich is on an unstable slope, so care is needed. At the head of this 'nose' is another ice carved lochan in a deep corrie – Lochan Gaineamhach, like so many of its kind is a sheer joy to look at, as the craigs and steep slopes that ring it, appear to drop straight into the sheet of water. There is no shore or transition from the one to the other, and at 738m, it is a high level lochan. The ascent however is up a fine shoulder of Sgurr a'Chaorachain

(1,053m) *peak of the little field of berries* mid-way along an exceptionally fine ridge with four prominent tops on the northern head of Loch Monar. The going is rocky, but otherwise firm. So turn right to Sgurr Choinnich (999m) *moss peak;* a very puzzling name, for there would appear to be little moss hereabouts – rock rules.

This is a place to pause and appreciate the fine surrounding vistas. Loch Monar meanders eastwards, its shores hemmed in tightly by the steep hills that flank it, and points towards Glen Strathfarrar. To the south, the bold rounded summit of An Cruachan marks a turning point in the Watershed's route further south, for it has taken a loop round Loch Calavie, by Beinn Dronaig. The view west over Attadale Forest is of a landscape dotted with lochans, and with Loch Carron tidal shores beyond.

The final Watershed section on this walk, involves a steep, but strangely rewarding descent to the Bealach Bhearnais which at 640m is a high level, but traditional local crossing. A short craggy ascent to yet another very fine ridge hill, Beinn Tharsuinn (863m) *transverse hill,* forms an arc round Coire Beithe, and with three marked tops, 817 followed by the 863 summit, and finally 795. Along the way a lochan on the ridge provides a delightful place to pause, and to wonder at its very presence so high up. The terrain is a delight to walk on, firm short grasses dotted with a carpet of wild flowers. At this point you leave the Watershed, which now takes a southerly course, as described above.

The Exit

This is best achieved by returning to the Bealach Bhearnais along Beinn Tharsuinn. Drop north to the Allt Leathad an Tobair, and picking up the path which leads to the bridge and then the estate track down the Allt a'Chonais glen. This in turn leads to the bridge crossing of the River Carron, and back to Craig.

Walk 20 The Splendour of Beinn Dearg and Seana Bhraigh
Sheet 20
Distance 39km (0 : 28 : 11) – 19hrs,
or 44km – 21hrs
Access by bus

To do this walk justice will require a full two day outing, and onto some of the most popular tops in this part of the country. Beinn Dearg is a familiar sight, for all who journey towards Ullapool, and perhaps the ferry to Lewis. As you pass Loch Glascarnoch, you become aware of this great bulwark of a mountain rearing up on the right, before crossing the Watershed and descending the Dirrie More to Loch Broom. It is a mountain with purpose.

Or, if you approach Ullapool from the other side, from Coigach, and round the bend where the road to Rhue turns off, there is an exceedingly fine skyline behind the town. Ullapoll has some magnificent mountains in its back yard. But this is of course only part of the story, because some of the mountains on this walk are tucked away, and await discovery the energetic way.

Two mountains stand out amongst all the rest on this most appealing of routes – Beinn Dearg (1,084m) and Seana Bhraigh (927m).

Obstacles   2 fences, few sheep, and some beasts on the lower ground.

The Access

This walk starts right on the Watershed at Spot 279 on the A835 at the east end of Loch Droma, aptly, *loch of the ridge.*

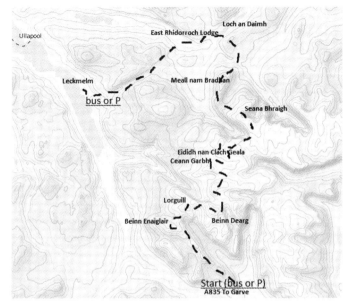

Route Map 20

There is a good bus service from Inverness to Ullapool, which can be used to get to the start, however advanced on-line or Tourist Information Centre booking is strongly recommended.

The Walk

To get to this point the Watershed has come from Beinn Liath Bheag, following a very fine route through the group of mountains that are affectionately referred to by many, as The Fannichs.

From spot 279, the route follows a ridge heading north-west by a couple of spot heights, 497 and 519 to Meall Feith Dhiongaig (535m). Just beyond, a somewhat rare feature on the Watershed occurs for the next two kilometres, a path, which has come up from Lochdrum; and it is here pretty much on the Watershed. The ridge continues with Meallan Mhurchaidh, and then soon enough, the path must be abandoned, in order to reach Beinn Enaiglair (889m) from which the view down Loch Broom is appealing. Drop to the north east to the col, crossing the earlier path, and a steep rocky ascent of Iorguill *hill of the turmoil or the battle* (872m) follows. Continue across a fine pavement terrain to spot 836, and turn east and pick up the dyke that marks the top of the 250m craigs. This dyke is a work of craftsmanship and engineering in stone; a magnificent structure. Although it appears to be leading to the summit of Beinn Dearg *red hill*, it veers off to the north round the head of the crags, so some careful route planning is called for to find the summit cairn at 1,084m; a formidable structure amongst a scatter of boulder, grit and solid rock.

With spot 886 as the next target, the descent is rough, and involves picking a way through a steep boulder field. The dyke re-appears from the left, and again acts as a good guide. Continuing in a horseshoe round the crag-girt head of Gleann na Sguaib, takes the route by yet more boulders to Meall nan Ceapraichean *hill of the stumps or hummocks* (977m), and then another loop to the right to Ceann Garbh (967m). This is a ridge, a great east west divide between Inverlael Forest on the left and Gleann Beag to the right. However, the route is a series of wide meanders, with a succession of steep sided valleys to be rounded. The route to and then beyond Eididh nan Clach Geala *web of white stones* (928m) is typical, and yet another sweep leads to Spot 863. A high level morass needs to be traversed safely to get to spot 806, which is in turn followed by firmer terrain at the top of the craigs round the head of the Cadha Dearg or *red pass*.

This has set the scene for that great favourite Seana Bhraigh *old slope* (927m), by way of spot 906, with more stunning craigs dropping steeply for some 350m to the right. The summit is marked by a small shelter ring of rough stone dyke. Time then, for a brew and view stop, for the panoramas are impressive.

A steady descent of over 350m in just one kilometre requires care, but it is generally on grass, with the odd boulder somehow defying gravity and clinging to the side of the hill. The ridge continues north with Creag Dhubh (592m) and Meall nam Bradhan (679m), and by a somewhat indirect line, to spot 353m. A final short stretch of Watershed by way of Mullach a'Bhreun-Leitir (406m) and crossing to the south of Loch an Daimh to the track at 257937, where you leave the Watershed, as it heads off into the intriguing Rhidorroch landscapes (see description in *Ribbon of Wildness*).

The Exit

Follow the track round to East Rhidorroch Lodge, and then follow the path south west through Srath Nimhe to Leckmelm and the A835.

Alternatively, the slightly longer track out by Loch Achall to Ullapool. This has the advantage of not needing to book and wait for public transport on the A835.

Walk 21 Across the Moine Thrust
Sheet 15
Distance 24.5km (2 : 17 : 5.5) – 12hrs
Access by car and bicycle

The theme of fine vantage points, and all of the superb views that these bring, is a continuing one, throughout this book. So too, is the way in which following the Watershed gives a powerful sense of place within the Scottish landscape, and the key geographic features which either relate to it, or can be appreciated from it. The place of the Watershed is without equal in the bigger Scottish landform.

The Moine Thrust is a geological feature running from south of Skye to Loch Eriboll on the north coast, and in which older rocks have been thrust and piled on top of younger layers. It is a low-angle fault, and the thrust zone is up to 10km in width. Its impact on the north-west landscapes is manifest, and has inspired the creation of the North West Highlands Geopark, the eastern boundary of which is generally close to the Watershed. Although the line of the Thrust is fairly straight, it has a marked deviation to the east on the area around Conival.

This description of the Moine Thrust is of necessity brief, but it serves to provide at least a hint at why some of the landscapes of north-west are of such interest. It also suggests that this part of the Watershed has features that have particular appeal, and which can be seen and experienced by those who venture on this particular walk.

Breabag (718m) and Conival (987m) will each make a lasting impression, for their contrast and distinctive rocky characters.

Obstacles   2 fences, no sheep or beasts.

This walk is best accomplished with either 2 cars, or a car and bicycle.

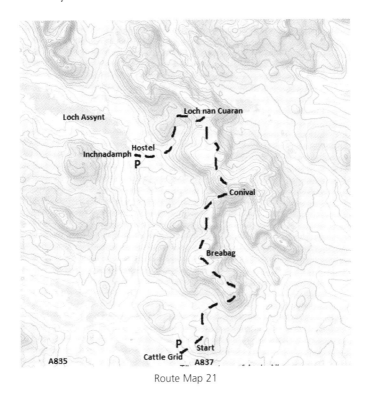

Route Map 21

The Approach

Travel on the A837 to Inchnadamph and park in the car park at the gate to Inchnadamph Hotel. Either leave one car, or a bicycle there. Drive south to the cattle grid at 278098, walk up the deer fence running north east, and join the Watershed as it emerges from the forest from spot 357 on its way to Ruighe Chnoc (369m).

The Walk

To reach this point, the Watershed has come from Seana Bhraigh to the south by way of Rhidorroch and the Cromalt Hills.

From Rhuigh Chnoc (369m), drop briefly and then climb north-east to Meall a'Bhraghaid on Sgonnan Mor. The ridge then picks up a north westerly direction by way of spot 688 and Bealach Choinich. The very rocky nature of the terrain will have become evident, and it is necessary to pick a way with care. This rough landscape is accentuated when, just after Meall Diamhain, the Coirean Ban opens up to the right. Find spot 815 and then Fuarain Ghlasa, and passing lochans on either side you are then on the spectacular rock strewn landscape of Breabag (718m). This is a rare place; wide and in places almost like a vast shallow basin with huge rocks and areas of pavement and slab, that is like no other. Two big corries on the right drop raggedly towards the River Oykel over 400m below. The seemingly improbable presence of some lochans mark the way on either side to spot 659 and Breabag Tarsuinn as the finale to this immensely appealing mountain.

Conival, the next objective rears up to the north, after a

steep drop into the bealach that decisively marks the way. The ascent to Conival (987m) *hill of the dog*, is one of the most hazardous on the Watershed, and should be done with great care. It involves a very steep 400m climb through scree, boulder, craig, and the occasional grassy ledge. It should not be underestimated, but is a much safer proposition going up, rather than down – hence the direction proposed for this walk.

A brewstop on the summit will treat you to an exceptional panorama round the full compass.

South over Breabag and into the Strath Oykel is marked out by contrast; the former is almost devoid of vegetation and the rock-scape has a truly distinctive character. The blocks of dark green coniferous plantations beyond stand out rather starkly against the wild areas of open moor and hill surrounding them. Westwards is a very watery land-scape, but with some striking hills erupting from the sur-rounding moor; Suilven, Canisp, and Quinag, to name but three. The theme of lochs continues to the north, and is then followed with the distant Carn Dearg and Ben Hee (see Walk 22) giving a real interest to the horizon. Whilst to the west, a preview of the flow country is evident, north of the shoulder of Ben More Assynt.

Descending northwards from the summit of Conival, scree tumbles steeply to both left and right, and spot 860, just right of the Watershed is like a bastion with ramparts dropping away for 300m on three sides. These craigs continue for a further 1.5km, and when Loch nan Cuaran is reached, you leave the Watershed.

It of course continues its wild journey northwards to Beinn Leoid, and to that north-west turning on Carn Dearg (see Walk 22).

The Exit

Walk round to the south of Loch nan Cuaran, pick up the path that crosses the Allt Tarsuinn and then drops by way of the Allt Poll an Droighinn to Inchnadamph. Then reclaim your car and bicycle.

Walk 22   A Rocky Loop in the North West
Sheet 16
Distance 23km (2 : 16.5 : 4.5) – 10 hours
Access by car

This particular walk incorporates a major turning point in the Watershed as a whole, for the route has been largely northward in direction for hundreds of kilometres; the many meanderings have at least all added up to a journey north. In this group of hills in the far north-west however it sweeps round in a tight horseshoe, which here involves traveling south for 6km. But as the Watershed then drops steeply off Ben Hee, it gives at least a hint at the new direction – to the east, and then as if to really confuse, sets a course for a further 11km southwards. All the points of the compass are fully employed in this knot of hills.

Although it is a tight grouping, this walk is none the less in two parts. The first prowls round a formidable ridge hill running north south, called A'Ghlaise; this is at its heart, and it is visible throughout. The second part of the route is to Ben Hee to the east; following a steep drop to the bealach that caries the track to the remote Gobernuisgach Lodge. But Ben Hee is a definitive point of transition from the Moine March to the Northlands; it is the last major rocky encounter, before the flow country. The average elevation on the Moine has been around 595m, whereas that of the Northland is only about 240m. The word Hee and Tee (see walk 15), have the same root, and both mean the *Fairy Hill*.

Carn Dearg (797m), Beinn Direach (688m) and Ben Hee (873m) are in every sense the high points on this day which excels for its place on the Watershed, and the wider landscape context.

Obstacles 2 fences, no sheep and no beasts.

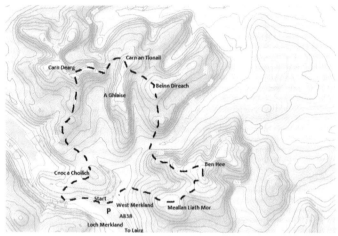

Route Map 22

The Access

Travel on the A838 Lairg to Laxford Bridge road and park at West Merkland. Walk west to spot 144, and join the Watershed.

The Walk

To reach this point, the Watershed has come from the south west, from Conival, by way of Beinn Leoid and Creag an Sgamhlainn, before a steep descent through native woodland to the road.

The walk starts with a modest climb to Cnoc a'Choilich (374m), skirting a young plantation en-route. Picking a route across some wetter ground between Loch Eas na Maoile and the Allt Beithe, the ground then firms-up on the climb to Meallan Liath Beag – *lump of the little grey hill*. This in turn leads onto the pronounced spur of Carn Dearg, with Loch Ulbhach Coire far below on the right, and the impressive Creag na h-Uidhe side of A'Ghlaise beyond. A very fine curved ridge leads both on and off Carn Dearg (797m) *red hill*, with a sweep of rough craigs dropping very steeply to the north. Well worth a pause here, to take in the scene. The nearest tarmac road to the north is that which rounds the head of Loch Eriboll, is over 15km distant, and the terrain, though crossed by two lonely estate paths is distinctively wild. Cape Wrath is some 35km away to the north-west, with only one road-crossing, and in the interim, there is a collection of hills that are nothing, if not iconic for the keen climber. Almost devoid of vegetation, rock is all, on Arkle, Foinaven, and around the slopes and screes of Strath Dionard. But these must wait for another venture. Westwards, the view is over Reay Forest and environs, with Loch More and Loch Stack catching the light, whilst salt water at Loch Glendhu is but a dozen kilometres away. And the profile of Ben More Assynt dominates the southern horizon. These few features are of course only a tiny part of the picture, but they help to place our Watershed in the much wider landscape, and upon the map of Scotland.

The route skirts round Lochan a'Bhealaich by spot 582, as a precursor to a steady 200m ascent to Carn an Tionail (759m) *hill of the gathering,* which is at the northern end of the A'Ghlaise ridge – it may mean *the greyness,* but it is far from drab. A succession of ups and downs follow, with Beinn Direach (688m) – *upright or straight hill*, Ceann Garbh na Beinne Direich *rough head of the upright hill,* and Meall a'Chleirich (628m); these names speak volumes about the terrain, and about just how our ancestors both viewed and experienced it. Meanwhile, to the left, you have passed the head of the very aptly named Coire Granda, and then a long steep drop into Bealach nam Meirleach *the robbers pass,* with that track to Gobernuisgach. Descend with care to spot 266 on the track.

Sail Garbh *rough heel* with its twin tops of 582 and 677 involves another steady 300m ascent, and the craigs on her north face appear to drop, decisively, to Loch an Tuim Bhuidhe far below. The climb to Ben Hee *the fairy hill* (873m), is interrupted here and there by slabs of rock seeming to stick awkwardly out of the ground, in the same way as those experienced on Trowgrain Middle (see Walks 2 and 3). But the sense of anticipation is heightened as the summit is attained, for the curtain has dropped, and a wide landscape been revealed. This is an important landscape, with a succession of designated areas stretching east over bog, moor and hill – the primary focus of this is bog-land, but no ordinary marsh is this. The citation for this area proclaims: 'The Peatlands of Caithness and Sutherland form the largest and most intact area of blanket bog in Scotland'. It is a rare peatland type, in world terms. Much of it is SSSI, and in total, there are 143,569 ha that are designated and protected as Ramsar sites. Further and more detailed information on this is contained in *Ribbon of Wildness.*

A white dot on the moorlands to the south west is the Crask Inn (see Walk 23). The hills beyond are much more rounded in form than those on the earlier part of this walk, with the bulk of Ben Klibreck and Ben Armine then rolling off to the south. Loch Shin, Strath Grudie and Glen Cassley all point the way to Strath Oykel. And a multitude of lochs, both great and small dominate the landscapes to the north east. Ben Hee is a delightful vantage point.

You leave the Watershed at this point, as it continues by Ben Hee's unnamed northern top, and then drops onto the start of the flow country, by Cnoc an Alaskie, The Crask and beyond.

The Exit

Descent is to the west by Meallan Liath Mor (683m), and directly, if steeply, to West Merkland.

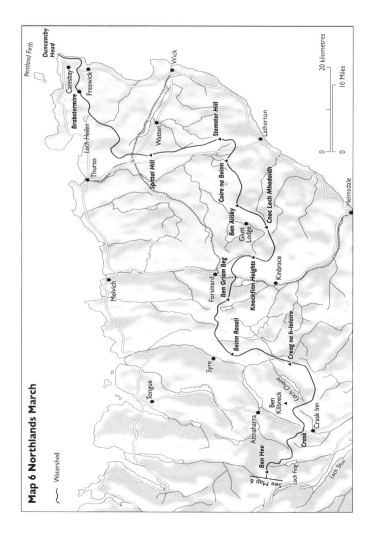

Map 6 Northlands March

~ Watershed

Pentland Firth

Duncansby Head

Canisbay

Brabstermire

Freswick

Loch Heilen

Wick

Thurso

Watten

Spittal Hill

Stemster Hill

Latherton

Coire na Beinn

Croc Loch Mhadaidh

Helmsdale

Ben Alisky

Glutt Lodge

Melvich

Forsinard

Ben Griam Beg

Knockfinn Heights

Kinbrace

Beinn Rosail

Creag na h-Iolaire

Syre

Tongue

Loch Choire

Ben Klibreck

Crask Inn

Altnaharra

Crask

Ben Hee

See Map 6

Loch a' Ghoil

Loch Shin

20 kilometres

10 Miles

The Northlands March (3)

TO VENTURE UPON the Northlands March of the Watershed of Scotland is to experience a landscape with its very own character and scale. Yes, we have encountered bog and moorland on earlier walks, but the scale of it here in these parts of Sutherland and Caithness is quite unique. Any misconceptions about bleakness or flatter monotony, which some might nurture about this area, should be cast aside without further ado.

The ruggedness that had been so familiar on Moine and Heartland is behind us now, and is replaced here with a much subtler drama. This is the landscape of colour and richness, of movement and texture, of gentler slope, the dancing light, and the wide skies. Neil Gunn, the mid 20th-century local author, evocatively captured all of this, and so much more in his novels. The name that I have chosen for this March – The Northlands, is drawn from his heart and hand; he would have been pleased with this accolade.

It is hard now to imagine the battle for the peatlands that raged some 25 years ago, about the importance and need for conservation of these habitats, but the rage was both vocal and vociferous. At issue was the way in which the tax system enabled, nay encouraged, the wealthy in other parts of the UK, to buy up large tracts of 'low cost and poor quality peat bog', plant it with sitka, and benefit greatly from this through perfectly legal 'tax efficiency'. Tax avoidance for the wealthy, and PAYE for the rest of us, perhaps! But there was rapidly growing awareness of the singular qualities of this, the Flow

Country; appreciation by a wider and articulate public of the rich and diverse habitats that were systematically being destroyed by this ill-conceived fiscal system. This area was beginning to stand out both nationally and internationally as distinctive and in urgent need of rigorous protection. And thus it was, by every means possible. European and national legislation was employed to designate and protect, the pernicious tax regime was addressed, the RSPB and other key agencies got actively involved, and the conservation of the Flow Country had begun in earnest.

Although the tide of destruction has turned in many parts of the Flow Country, others have been lost to the sitka and all that that represents. But much of the Northlands March has survived, and provides a superb vantage point from which to view and experience. The hill and moorland areas make for relatively easy going, but bog is never far from the route. Those areas of 'flow', or raised peatbog, which include pools of open water, dubh lochans, or a wet surface mat of loose vegetation, are manifest in a number of locations; they are both a delight, and a challenge. The final approach to Duncansby Head is across grassland, moor, and by clifftop; it has a genuine sense of anticipation about it. For it is either the second last in an impressive list of these chosen walks, or the conclusion of an epic on the Mainland of Scotland; either way, it brings the Northlands March to a very fine finale.

Or does it though? For I offer a tantalising glimpse of what lies beyond, the Viking March, but more of that, anon.

Walk 23   The Crask
Sheet 16
Distance 30km (1 : 15.5 : 13.5) – 12 hours
Access by car

'It's a long way from Peel Fell' was one of the thoughts that came to me as I tried, somewhat in vain, to avoid the midges, and made my way the short distance from The Crask *the crossing*, to the Crask Inn north of Lairg in the summer of 2005. As I looked at the map of Scotland that evening in the (midge free) Inn and after a substantial meal cooked and presented by Kai and Mike, I did find it hard to believe that I had indeed walked all that way – of well over a thousand kilometres. I'd done some real bog hopping that day though on an extensive and fine example of flow country; I was I felt, getting the hang of it. But I knew there was still much bog to beat. Fond memories of a special place with special people, and at a key point somehow in the epic. So it is only right to share it with a wider public and contrive a walk that will give a real flavour for the place.

Often described as the 'road that goes up the middle', by Lairg and Altnaharra to Tongue on the north coast of Scotland, the A836 is rarely busy. Munroists will be familiar with it, because it gives access to that outlier Ben Klibreck. This walk has been plotted as a figure-of-eight outing that will combine more Watershed than not, some hill, a nice wee flavour of the flows in a remote spot, and a walk back beside two delightful lochs.

This is a walk of 'almosts' – onto the shoulder of Ben Klibreck, but not to the summit, and just about into the Ben Armine Forest area. But this detracts in no way from the delights which Cnoc Sgriodain (544m) and Meall an Fhuarain (504m) will present.

Obstacles   3 fences, few sheep, and a few beasts.

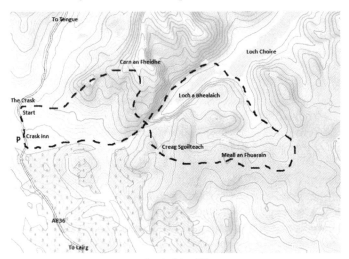

Route Map 23

The Access

Travel on the A836 north of Lairg, and park at the Crask Inn. Walk north to The Crask at spot 264, and join the Watershed.

The Walk

To reach this point the Watershed has come from the north-west from Ben Hee (see walk 22), by way of Creag Dhubh

Mhor, Cnoc an Alaskie, and some formidable flow country terrain.

Walk and climb to the north east onto Cnoc Sgriodain (544m), and Carn an Fheidh. Turn south by spot 528 to the Bealach Easach *bealach of the horse* crossing. Continue south east to Creag Sgoilteach (471m) with Loch Gaineamhach on your left. This is a good place to stop and get a real sense of place. The great long whaleback of Ben Klibreck fills the view to the north – this is an outlier for those who are tackling the Munros, as the nearest, Ben Hope, is some distance away to the north-west. The waters of Loch a'Bhealaich and Loch Choire nestle some 780m below the ridges and craigs which protrude from the south side of the Ben. Whilst the hillsides on the south sides of these lochs are delightfully clothed in areas of native woodland. Ben Armine and its erstwhile Forest lies to the east, with lochans and flow scattered throughout the landscape. The view south down Strath Tirry towards Lairg, is something of a disappointment, as it includes a large area of somewhat scraggy commercial forest. But raise your eyes to the west and north, and the 24km light catching length of Loch Shin points to some more mountainous areas at its head, and the profiles of Ben More Assynt and Ben Hee make a dramatic skyline.

The route continues across some flow (a modest introduction) to Meall an Fhuarain (503m). Spots 487 and 596 will take you across some gently undulating moorland. Turn left onto the track just beyond, and leave the Watershed.

The Watershed continues from this point, to Creag na h-Iolaire and Meall nan Aighean, before descending to Truderscaig.

The Exit

Follow the track north west, passing the remains of the pre-clearance settlement of Fearna, to the junction of the two lochs, where a strategically placed bridge will enable you to cross to the north side. There, the path climbs to re-cross the Watershed at the Bealach Easach, and continues alongside the River Tirry by the Strath a'Chraisg to the Crask Inn.

Walk 24 Forsinard and The Flows
Sheets 17 and 10
Distance 34km (8 : 13.5 : 12.5) – 15hrs
Access by car or train

The Flow Country, that vast area of north Sutherland and Caithness which contains so many areas of peat bog, is not just of importance in the Scottish or UK context, but on the world stage too. It was for a time being systematically destroyed by a tax avoidance (efficiency) scheme that the wealthy were able to freely exploit, by planting large areas of non-native trees. This involved draining the land to lower the water table prior to the planting, through both activities, altering the entire eco-system, and driving away many rare species, especially of bird life. Peatlands are of particular ecological importance, and nowhere more-so than here.

Much of the Flow Country straddles the Watershed, and whilst it can be extremely difficult in some place to plot the precise route, largely on account of the many areas of what could be referred to as indecisive water, which can't make up its mind which way to go, close scrutiny of the OS maps has finally produced a meandering line which is as near as it is ever likely to be, to defining the Watershed through this area.

So a walk which ventures into and onto some flow areas is a must, amongst this very varied collection. Forsinard is the focus of this outing, and walkers will be able to get a vivid picture of why and how these areas are now protected, and of the immensely rich variety of wildlife that they support or are now thankfully returning. Almost the entire flow country is now protected within the legislation that has led to the creation of Ramsar sites, sssi's, Special Areas of Conservation, and National Scenic Areas. Bird life is central to all of this, and the work of the RSPB of great importance. From late April to mid-June, during the nesting seasons of a number of different species, walkers are asked to follow the route given here, and to keep on the move – other than at the higher points where a pause and a good view can readily be enjoyed.

The two hills that dominate this route through an iconic landscape, with its rich habitats, are Meall a'Bhealaich (337m) and Ben Griam Beag (580). Neither is especially big, but their place and prospect are immense.

Obstacles   4 fences, one railway, no sheep and no beasts.

This is either one very long day walk, or two shorter and more leisurely outings.

The Access

Travel on the A897 to Forsinard station and park beside the RSPB visitor centre. It is well worth taking time to visit the centre, to discover the importance of the flows, and the work of the RSPB in conserving them. Exit onto the road, turn left, and cross the railway. Pick up the forest track to the left heading south east, and walk beyond the bend at 924396 to the second of the two burns, the Allt na Claise Moire. Turn right up this burn, and exit the forest after about 1km. Travel south to trig point at spot 438, and join the Watershed.

Route Map 24

The Walk

To get to this point, the Watershed has come from Ben Alisky, by Cnoc Loch Mhadaidh and Cnoc Maol-dhuin. This trig point closely overlooks a very fine area of pools and peatland above Knockfin Heights – one of the finest parts of the flow country and is an area that has almost as much open water as there is vegetation mat. Now turn north by the west side of spot 387 and Cnoc Riabhach, and continue north-west to Cnoc nam Bo Riabhach. A suitable gap in the trees then takes you by a gentle ascent to Meall a'Bhealaich (337m), and it's all too prominent mast. But turn your back on it, for this is a good place to survey the scene. To the north, Strath Halladale stretches out towards Melvich on the Atlantic coast. To the south and east, Strath of Kildonan (otherwise known as Strath Ullie) takes the Helmsdale River to the village of the same name, on the North Sea coast. The scene is somewhat marred by the line of pylons, the origin of which was the former Dounreay Nuclear Power Station. But ignoring this intrusion, there is evidence of areas of very wet peat bog in almost every direction. The pair of dominant Griam hills stands out boldly from this to the west; although one is the Mor and the other the Beg, there is only 10m between them in elevation.

Descend, towards the disused gravel pit beside the A897 and aim to cross it at spot 177. This is a slight deviation, but is recommended by the RSPB. Your next goal in a somewhat indirect way is Ben Griam Beg, but first the railway, and them some flow must be crossed. Pass to the north of the small area of pools beside spot 175 and the cairn, and then to the south of the much larger area of pools. Keep Cnoc Bad an Amair (233m) in sight; the bog-hopping should be minimised, but will not be without some excitement. Turn sharp left, and passing the pool beside spot 214 skirt the remains of the forest to ascend steeply between the tops of Ben Griam Beg. A right turn will then take you to the top at 580m, the trig point and the remains of a substantial fort structure. Clearly this was a significant place in days gone by; a perfect place for a brew-view.

The land to the west is similar to Rhidorroch. It is chaotic and almost devoid of any apparent structure – the burns seem to flow hither and thither, there are lochans dotted around the strange landscape, and even the minor areas of higher ground bear no relation one with the other. To the north, the superb work of the RSPB is evident; where areas of trees have been felled, and drains blocked in an effort to restore the habitats that preceded the coming of the sitka. Lurking behind the larger of the Griams lies the loch with three names, or in three parts – Badanloch, Nan Clar and Rimsdale.

Although the descent is to the west from the summit of the hill, it may be prudent to make a slight detour to avoid the craigs. In any event, it will be steep, before the flatter turn to the north-west to find spot 314. The route then turns westward between Loch Gaineimh on the left and the irregularly shaped Loch Crocach on the right, with Cnoc nan Tri-chlach (345m) *hill of the three stones* in your sights. At this point you leave the Watershed.

The Watershed continues from here in the direction of Creag na h-lolaire near Ben Armine, but the route there is a very meandering one indeed.

The Exit

Travel north to spot 347, then east to spot 291, and the forest edge before spot 256. Pick up the forest tracks heading east towards Cnoc a Bhreun-bhaid, followed by a path to Forsinard Lodge. Turn right to reach the visitor centre at the station.

Walk 25   Guard of Honour at Duncansby Head

Sheet 12
Distance 23km (2.5 : 18 : 2.5) – 9hrs
Access by car and bus

This walks collection would be incomplete without a day out to Duncansby. Thousands of people walk, cycle, ride and roller skate to John O' Groats, ostensibly as the top right hand corner of the UK, having travelled from Land's End, at the other end. That JO'G gets all the attention is perhaps just as well, for it leaves Duncansby in relative peace, and to be enjoyed more fully by those who venture along and to the cliff-top headland.

For those who walk the whole (mainland) Watershed from the Peel Fell, this is journey's end, with all of the sense of triumph and elation that that would bring. It points tantalisingly to Orkney (see Walk 26) and to a possible continuation northwards to walk and sail eventually to Muckle Flugga on the Island of Unst and its views over the Norwegian Sea. But that is for another day, perhaps. For the majority who have walked their own selection of Watershed walks though, this would be a fitting one, if not to end on, then to make sense of it all at least, for from Duncansby you can see the North Sea and the Atlantic Ocean, whilst standing in the one place and with just a turn of the head. Here alone you can see what it's been about, including the wildness. Paradoxically, this will be the least strenuous of this collection of walks. However, it should be noted that it includes a number of extensive areas of moor and moss, which can be tough going. These are enlivened however, with small collections of enchanting lochans near the middle, fringed with lilies, and attracting a range of bird life.

This is a walk with few hills, but Mounthalie (72m), Brabster (87m) and Warth Hill (124m) will most assuredly repay a pause on the route, with a gripping sense of place.

Obstacles 8+ fences, some sheep, and some beasts.

Route Map 25

The Access

Travel on the A836 to the Burn of Midsands car park on the north side of the road. Then cross the road with care, there is a gate in the fence on the north side of the road, about 100m east of the bridge, and walk south by the Links of Greenland, keeping the burn and dyke on your right. This area is generally machair, easy to walk on, and dotted with all of the wild flowers that you would associate with this terrain. Pick up the track to Lower Greenland, and continue south east to Greenland Mains and the Mounthalie Cottage at the top of the hill. You join the Watershed at Mounthalie (72m).

Note: there is a bus service from Thurso to John O' Groats, which passes Burn of Midsands car park, every two hours or so, Monday to Saturday.

The Walk

To get to this point the Watershed has taken a meandering route from Sordale Hill, having come north for some distance roughly parallel with the A9, from Stemster Hill.

Walk east for some 4km to the forest just short of Slickly, and turn north east and take a bearing for Hill of Slickly (73m). Continue on this bearing for a further 3km to 315704, and turn east again, to the mast beside spot 87. Take a bearing for spot 73 on the U road 3km to the east. Ascend Giar Hill, and go south east to Warth Hill (124m). Cross the A99 at spot 99 and head just to the south of Loch of Lomashion, reaching the cliff top north of Fast Geo. Follow the highest point close to the cliff top by Hill of Crogodale (76m) and continue north east to journey's end at the lighthouse.

Although some parts of this walk are over somewhat featureless terrain, the range of wild flowers which grow hereabouts is outstanding. In season it is a sheer delight to count the many different varieties that flourish in this landscape, and if you can identify them, so much the better. The birdlife is rich and varied too, and if you can spot that skylark that is pouring out that musical torrent, you are doing well. The views north across the Pentland Firth to the cliffs of Hoy and the gentler coast of South Ronaldsay beckon in a rather tantalising manner, and you cannot see the Island of Stroma without being struck by the hard existence that its former residents endured. Were sea levels to drop (yes, an unlikely scenario), the link with Orkney would be by way of an arc from Duncansby Head to Little Skerry and Muckle Skerry en-route to Brough Ness on South Ronaldsay.

The Stacks of Duncansby stand out like a guard of honour

for your final few kilometres of this walk to Duncansby Head, and as your route rounds the head of Geo of Sclaites, the Watershed is but a foot wide. Yes, the final approach to the lighthouse is an immensely rewarding experience. Groome's Ordnance Gazetteer of Scotland of 1884 firmly nailed the northern terminus of the Watershed of Scotland to this point; we can now experience and enjoy every bit of the 1,200km meander all the way from Peel Fell on the Border. Scotland's very own ribbon of wildness.

The Exit

Walk by the road or the north coast cliff top to John O' Groats, and either reclaim the car that you left there earlier, or take the service bus back to the Midsands car park at Dunnet Bay, if that is where you have left your car.

Walk 26   On the Mainland of Orkney
Sheet 6
Distance 31.5km (1 : 31 : 0.5) – 13 hours
Access by Ferry, car and bus

This walk may appear to be something of an extra, for it lies beyond the standard Watershed on the mainland of Scotland. However, the place of both Orkney and Shetland are key to determining the northern terminus of the Watershed of Scotland at Duncansby Head; these island groups help to reaffirm the simple business of the destination of rain water landing, and its journey to either the North Sea, or the Atlantic Ocean. This principal is of course explored in greater detail elsewhere, and the Orkney and Shetland dimension to it is set firmly as part of the bigger picture. By poring over the sea-charts to discover the shallowest crossings from the mainland and from one island to the next, it has been possible to plot the continuation of the Watershed through these islands. This route is alluded to in *Ribbon of Wildness*, and offers a tantalising hint at a very legitimate journey by water and land all the way to Muckle Flugga at the northern tip of Shetland.

Whilst much of that is for another day, this walk along some of the higher ground on the Mainland of Orkney, will however provide a journey into another, altogether different landscape; one that is filled with very accessible pleasure and delight. Almost 20km of this walk is across two sites that combine SSSI and Special Protection Area status.

In this land of the wide skies, even the most modest of hill affords the pleasure of a fine vista. Wideford Hill (225m), Mid Tooin (221m) and Burgar Hill (159m), will each in their

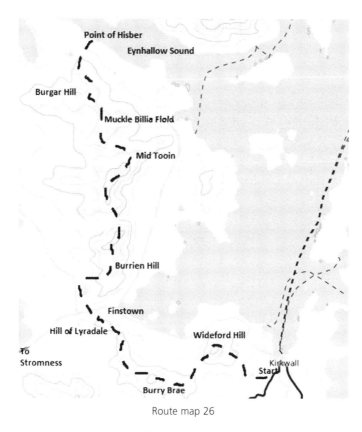

Route map 26

turn, and with much of what lies between them, provide a compelling image of the wider Orkney sea-landscape.

The Access

Travel north to Caithness, and then by ferry from either Scrabster, John o' Groats or Gills Bay to the Mainland of Orkney. Kirkwall will make an excellent base for this walk. Walk south west from the centre of Kirkwall to the A964, and join the Watershed at about the Youth Hostel. Exploring the town will have to wait, but it has much to be explored and experienced – from St Magnus Cathedral to the Highland Park Distillery, a narrow winding street to the Bishop's Palace, it will not be hard to while away a day or two very purposefully. Meantime though, back to the Watershed.

The Walk

To get to this point the Watershed has come north by way of Pentland Skerries, South Ronaldsay, and crossing the Churchill Barriers to the Holm part of the main island.

Walk west by Corse, cross the U road at Sunnybank, and ascend Wideford Hill (225m). On the way, one or two of those distinctive Orkney fences will prove a challenge to be endured, but of course 'practice makes perfect', so the effort is not wasted. The summit of Wideford Hill has been well and truly sullied, by a plethora of masts and associated buildings, but turn your back on this clutter, move round and just take-in the Orkney landscape and seascapes. The gentle heather clad hills, green fields below, and ever changing moods of the water will captivate.

Turn south west, re-crossing the U road close top Smerquoy, and head for Burrey Brae (148m). From here the wide expanse of Scapa Flow opens out to the south; now the favourite haunt of divers and fishermen, it played a major strategic role in both world wars. To the left a marker buoy identifies the watery grave of so many brave sailors who lost their lives with the sinking of the Royal Oak HMS by a German U Boat. To the right, the Hills of Hoy *high island*, contrast with the softer profile of much of the rest of Orkney. The route then goes west over heather moors by way of Keellylang Hill (221m), Hill of Lyradale (176m) and then north-west to Hill of Heddle (135m). There is water on both sides, with Wide Firth to the north, and the ever changing sea moods of Scapa Flow to the south; it is beguiling. Descend to the A965 to cross at spot 37 – a few rough fields on either side of the road soon give way to some moor and wetlands. Then, travel north, with Loch of Wasdale on the right almost as far as Lunan, before turning east to Burrien Hill.

As you climb, look back from time to time, and you will become aware of the huge basin that forms much of this part of the Mainland; dominated by two lochs, one salt-water and the other fresh, with a ring of hills almost surrounding the whole. In the middle of it lies a complex of ancient standing stones and burial mounds which combine to give the prized UNESCO World Heritage Site accolade. Whilst all around, are yet more islands and sounds, lochans with their dancing light and those wide open moors, with the skylark pouring her exquisite refrain in praise of it all, or so it seems.

The route is then northwards by the lochs at Verigend and crossing the U road at Chair of Lyde. The three Tooins follow, with Ernie coming first, then Tooin of Rush, followed by Mid Tooin (221m), with its trig point. A number of minor meanders then take the route to Little Billia Field, Starling Hill, Starra Fiold, Muckle Billia Fiold, the upper part of

Quinni Moan, and the U road at Breeran. Blythemo comes in quick succession, and with the wind farm now dominating the scene. These moors are still used for cutting peats for domestic fuel – a back breaking task, which casts some doubt on just how 'free' this fuel really is. The going is quite tough in places, with the long ungrazed heather and peat banks to be encountered. The Wards is followed by the RSPB reserve on Lowrie's Water to the left, and finally Burgar Hill (159m). Gradually, a new panorama has unfolded across Eynhallow Sound to Rousay and a further collection of small islands; beyond the low lying Stronsay, the North Sea widens to complete the distant eastern horizon. Open sea to the west, is of course, the Atlantic Ocean in all its marine majesty. Twice in every 24 hours their respective tides battle it out in the channel below, where all the sights sounds of a river in full flood provide an impressive image of the immense power of nature.

The Watershed route then descends to the north east by Feolquoy, crossing the A966 at spot 36 at Burgar. Finally, aim for the Broch and Point of Hisber on the shore.

The Watershed continues across the Eynhallow Sound to The Graand on the one side of the island, and the skerries north of Fint, on the other, before picking up again, on Rousay, and onwards.

The Exit

Retrace to Burgar on the A966 where there are five public service busses a day, midweek, and a reduced service at week-ends. This will then take you back to Kirkwall via Tingwall and Finstown.

Time for Reflection

THERE CAN BE NO single feature that captures the spirit and character of the whole Scottish landscape, no one place that is in any way typical, or even the most general phrase to adequately describe it. Scotland is certainly the sum of its parts, and as such encompasses a wide variety of terrain; lowland and highland, coast and moor, forest and field, urban and rural, and much more besides. It is of course this endless variety that makes it all so appealing, and ensures that there is something for everyone who ventures to find a favourite or special place. To get tuned in to nature's bounty is to be rich indeed.

As you have read through these pages, and then perchance, donned your boots for an outing or two on the Watershed, you will have been touched or even uplifted by a little of this great ribbon of wildness. Hopefully you will have felt some connection with this one geographic feature which does include some of the best, finest and continuously wilder Scottish landscape throughout its mega meander.

The fuller picture of all this can be found in *Ribbon of Wildness*, and the best experience of it is to be out there enjoying it, as touched on here in *Walking with Wildness*. Nature alone put the Watershed there, its evolution has been slower than many of the changes we are accustomed to; it is surely Scotland's immense environmental gem; our sleeping giant.

Awareness about the special, unique even, qualities of the Watershed of Scotland is growing inexorably. People are getting many different things from this, each and every one is personal, and all are deeply enriched in some very worthwhile way.

Some other books published by **LUATH** PRESS

The East Highland Way

Kevin Langan
ISBN 978-1-908373-40-3 PBK £9.99

The East Highland Way is a detailed and descriptive guide to the route developed by Kevin Langan in 2007. Beginning in Fort William and culminating in Aviemore, the trail forms a new link route between the northern end of the West Highland Way and the southern end of the Speyside Way. In addition, the route joins with the Great Glen Way at its southern point in Fort William, making this an exciting new challenge for seasoned walkers and amateurs alike. Not only an illustrated route description, Langan also details the plethora of wildlife and historical attractions to be spotted along the way in each section of the walk.

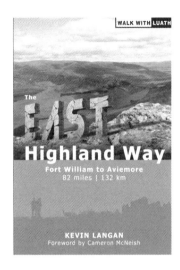

There is a real need for alternative routes and The East Highland Way offers not only an alternative, but a highly attractive and challenging walk in its own right.
CAMERON MCNEISH

The Ultimate Guide to the Munros Ralph Storer

Volume 1: Southern Highlands   ISBN 978-1-906307-57-8 PBK £14.99
Volume 2: Central Highlands South   ISBN 978-1-906817-20-6 PBK £14.99
Volume 3: Central Highlands North   ISBN 978-1-906817-56-5 PBK £14.99
Volume 4: Cairngorms South   ISBN 978-1-908373-51-9 PBK £9.99

 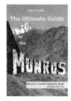 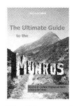 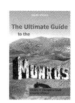

From the pen of a dedicated Munro bagger comes *The Ultimate Guide* to everything you've wished the other books had told you before you set off. The lowdown on the state of the path, advice on avoiding bogs and tricky situations, tips on how to determine which bump is actually the summit in misty weather... this series forms the only guide to the Munros you'll ever need.

These comprehensive rucksack guides feature:

Detailed descriptions of all practicable ascent routes up all the Munros and Tops in each region

Easy to follow quality and difficulty ratings

Annotated colour photographs and OS maps

The history of each Munro and Top

Notes on technical difficulties, foul-weather concerns, winter conditions and scenery

Winner of the highly commended Award for Excellence (for Vol. 1) by the Outdoor Writers and Photographics Guild

His books are exceptional... Storer subverts the guidebook genre completely.

THE ANGRY CORRIE

Irresistibly funny and useful... makes an appetising broth of its wit, experience and visual and literary tools. Brilliant.

OUTDOOR WRITERS AND PHOTOGRAPHICS GUILD

Details of these and other books published by Luath Press can be found at:
www.luath.co.uk

Luath Press Limited

committed to publishing well written books worth reading

LUATH PRESS takes its name from Robert Burns, whose little collie Luath (*Gael.,* swift or nimble) tripped up Jean Armour at a wedding and gave him the chance to speak to the woman who was to be his wife and the abiding love of his life. Burns called one of 'The Twa Dogs' Luath after Cuchullin's hunting dog in Ossian's *Fingal.* Luath Press was established in 1981 in the heart of Burns country, and now resides a few steps up the road from Burns' first lodgings on Edinburgh's Royal Mile.

Luath offers you distinctive writing with a hint of unexpected pleasures.

Most bookshops in the UK, the US, Canada, Australia, New Zealand and parts of Europe either carry our books in stock or can order them for you. To order direct from us, please send a £sterling cheque, postal order, international money order or your credit card details (number, address of cardholder and expiry date) to us at the address below. Please add post and packing as follows: UK – £1.00 per delivery address; overseas surface mail – £2.50 per delivery address; overseas airmail – £3.50 for the first book to each delivery address, plus £1.00 for each additional book by airmail to the same address. If your order is a gift, we will happily enclose your card or message at no extra charge.

Luath Press Limited
543/2 Castlehill
The Royal Mile
Edinburgh EH1 2ND
Scotland
Telephone: 0131 225 4326 (24 hours)
Fax: 0131 225 4324
email: sales@luath.co.uk
Website: www.luath.co.uk